ME AND MY TWO SONS

A JOURNEY OF HEALING

Karen Rooney

Price-Patterson Ltd.
Montreal, Canada

Printed in Canada

Cover design by Studio Melrose/Ted Sancton
Cover photo by Wayne Rooney, with special
    thanks to Matthew Dodd
Author's photo by Inga Hazel

Editor: Stuart Woods

Price-Patterson Ltd.
Canadian Publishers

ISBN 1-897336-06-3

*This book is dedicated to the
memory of the late*

Dr. James E. Gibbons

*of the
Montreal Children's Hospital.
He gave me hope.*

Contents

I mother loudly
Equally generous with hugs
as with stern tones and frowns
I feed my sons' souls and bodies with
the wisdom I have gleaned from
an endless line of Mothers
who came before
reaching to the begining
they are my memories
I am not alone

FOREWORD

There are two things I hope to achieve in writing this book. First would be that parents of healthy children truly appreciate the wondrous gift they have received. The second would be for all the parents of children with health problems to garner the strength and hope to cope.

This book is a personal account of an amazing journey filled with fear, joy and gratitude. It is based on the extraordinary story of the births and early years of my two sons. The first child, Matthew, was born otherwise healthy, albeit five weeks premature by Caesarian-section. Within six weeks he was hospitalized with a near fatal infection. While undergoing treatment he was diagnosed with a rare congenital defect called cystic lung. The surgeon performed a lobectomy (removal of the lower lobe of the left lung) seven weeks later and only three days before federal regulations enforced donor blood testing for HIV on December 1, 1985. Welcome to motherhood. Seven-and-a-half years later, enter son number two, Kyle. Different father, same hospital. I enjoyed twenty-four hours of ignorant bliss following the induced dry birth. Then the nursery staff noticed that Kyle was blue. He was encapsulated and taken by ambulance to the Montreal Children's Hospital Neonatal Intensive Care Unit. Diagnosis: a severe heart malformation known as tricuspid atresia with a septal ventrical defect (a valve missing and a hole in his heart). That little hole would save his life. He would undergo groundbreaking surgery and a second uncommon open-heart surgery before his third birthday. Kyle is now thirteen and a wonderful child. Matthew is twenty-one, six-foot-three and a loving, caring individual. This is the story of my two sons.

I
MATTHEW'S BIRTH
AND AFTERBIRTH

Even pigs sweat on a day like this. Early August and no one should be eight months pregnant and weigh over two hundred pounds in this sweltering heat. My incredible bulk had caused my flip-flops to become mere wafers between my swollen feet and the ground. My only remaining avenue of exercise was swimming – floating, actually. I was an expert floater. So expansive was my engorgement that on the most humid days my legs became insolent and refused to bend. My expected due date for the blessed event was Labour Day, an ill omen.

I needed the refreshing mountain breezes of the Alps, the bracing chill of an air conditioner. I hauled my bulk out of my apartment and waddled to my friend Diane's house to go subterranean. She had rented a Jack the Ripper movie, a bad idea considering my upcoming, unexpected C-section. "Hi," she said. "I'm heading to the bank but make yourself comfortable, or as close to that as you can." She eyed my midsection. I planted myself in her cold, damp basement to catch the flick with my feet up and ice cubes tinkling musically in my Canada Dry ginger ale.

Suddenly, I was alone in someone else's home, leaking all over the sofa and clueless about how to turn off the VCR or the upstairs radio, for that matter. It was terribly important to have quiet so I could think. Diane would be back any moment, and as a mother of three, she would know what to do.

Her recommendation: "Let's make a pot of tea and call Mike." My husband, dutiful as always, hurried over to pick me up, though not literally. Even with his towering stature of six-foot-five, the undertaking would have required a small crane. We went to our apartment so the expectant father could shower and prepare mentally for the birth. I folded laundry. "I'm hungry," he called from the bathroom. The next stop was the Wendy's drive-thru to fortify him with meat. I, on the other hand, could have nothing at all, as we had been taught in pre-natal class.

Over to the hospital we raced, where my gallant knight quickly located a wheelchair and plopped me in it.

"Which way is it?" he asked.

"I don't have a clue."

Every instruction learned in Lamaze class, even the directions to the delivery room, had vacated our collective brains as he then mistakenly whisked me to the postnatal ward. There, an efficient nurse, standing ramrod straight like a drill sergeant, turned us around, pointed down the hall and said, "You have to go through there before you can get to here."

My gut reacted much the same way it had when I had been perched at the craggy summit of the baby hill for my first taste of skiing. I remember peering down in a panic at the minute specks I knew to be other skiers far below. The same fear now rose in my throat, as I dimly comprehended that the baby would have to be extracted before I could earn my spot with those lucky new mothers guarded by the nurse in the postnatal ward.

Once we found the right place, I was ushered into a labour room to have my fluid tested to see if it was my bladder or my uterus that had sprung a leak. My uterus won. In strode the resident, an Iroquois maiden with a thick rope braid that could have dispersed flies with just one flick.

After careful examination she said, "The baby can't possibly have two heads, and we're going to need an ultrasound to find out if this is indeed a bottom I'm feeling where the head should be."

It was Friday, and what do all good hospital technicians do on a Friday afternoon? They go home. A very disgruntled fellow had to be recalled and he completed the test in record time and with minimum conversation.

Following the procedure, we not only knew the baby was going to be premature but breech as well. A Caesarian-section was scheduled, after the appendectomy already in progress, in the only operating room available on the weekend. Speaking of weekends, I was missing the Montreal Expos game – almost nothing had ever made me miss a baseball game before. A disheveled orderly with a Popeye tattoo on his wrist wheeled my gurney into the injection room for an epidural.

The anesthetist folded me over a pillow and said, "Relax." Why is it that whenever someone tells you to relax you become even more nervous? Did he really relish sticking that enormous needle in my spine?

"Don't move," he warned. "Don't look at it either."

I imagined that I would be instantly paralyzed if the good doctor missed his mark. As he filled me up with body-numbing fluid he also filled me in on the score of the game. The Expos were winning.

My obstetrician was away on a golfing vacation – I'm sure they offer Golf 101 in medical school. I was five weeks early and about to have my baby delivered by a strange man I'd never met. Maybe we should go grab a cup of coffee first and get acquainted? All my ruminating did not delay the inevitable; I was cut open and the baby was extracted. The doctor, who after many years of education and even more of experience, proudly announced, "He has outdoor plumbing." We named him Matthew John.

Giving birth was not quite the mystical experience that I had envisioned. As a surgical sheet was draped across my chest, I stared at a green wall for most of the procedure. But once Matthew was born, the nurse put him near my shoulder so I could see him. I remember a tiny little face and a lot of blood. After he was cleaned up and while I was sewn back up, the infant was inspected, poked and prodded, his limbs and appendage counted and recounted. Then his father gave him back to the harried nurses. My son was a healthy seven pounds, four ounces, or so we believed for a few brief weeks. A few of those ounces were not so healthy. His defect, cystic lung, could have gone undetected for many years and its discovery later would have had a devastating effect. Early detection would prove a godsend.

Baby safely delivered, I could now lie half-drugged on my plastic hospital mattress and develop bedsores. My visitors poured in, bearing gifts and bathing me in ever-escalating, exuberant compliments on the prince resting in the royal nursery.

"He's the most beautiful, charming and well-behaved baby ever to be born in the Western hemisphere," my mother-in-law gushed. I could barely focus on their well-meaning and loving faces. They appeared very distant as I viewed them through the slits of my leaden lids. Theirs was a joyful hysteria that I was unable to participate in. My husband's grandmother was still in town from England and was ecstatic to have been here for the premature birth of her first great-grandchild. She stood at the foot of my bed, small boned, wiry, and as always, wearing one of the same two dresses she had sewn in Fiji years before. Her snowy white hair was piled on her head in a complex design that bobbed as she patted my swollen toes. She repeatedly said, "You've done a fine job." I held my breath, closed my eyes and wished they would all disappear. Slowly I peeked as I exhaled, somehow I endured and eventually they drifted away to their jobs, trips and visits to the supermarket. I fell asleep.

I was not a fan of rooming-in. I wanted them to keep the baby in the nursery, reason being that I would surely get my fill of baby at home. I intended to feed him every four hours on their schedule and they could keep him for the grueling 1 a.m. feeding. The baby was cute and all, but I had just had major abdominal surgery and was barely able to turn over, never mind actually walk. Picture a giant sea turtle lying prostrate on its back on the beach.

My new pediatrician, Dr. Bergman, stepped in to see me. He was small and greasy and slunk over to my side. He perched on the chair next to me, pulled out a note pad and proceeded to sketch a canoe. Turning quickly to face me, he poked his pencil stub at the drawing and asked, "Anyone in your family have a head shaped like a kayak?" Bewildered, I could only shake my head in an emphatic no. He then added, "Matthew's head is too long and narrow and will need a steel plate implanted immediately. Not to worry, it will be replaced with a bigger one as he grows."

I began to shake. In a panic, I telephoned Mike and could only sob into the receiver as I attempted to explain what had happened. The weasely doctor scurried from the room, never to be seen again. Lucky for him, as there was over a foot difference in height and almost one hundred pounds between him and my ex-footballer husband, who was now speeding to the hospital to confront the little man.

The head nurse strode in pushing a wheelchair. "We're going for a ride," she informed me as she loaded me into the contraption. I was pushed to the preemie ward to view my son and to calm my fears. She said, "That doctor is crazy, he doesn't know what he's saying. Your baby is fine."

This kind, matronly woman proceeded to tell me that due to Matthew's positioning in the womb his soft skull had temporarily been squished. He had been bent completely in half with a foot behind each ear for at least three months. "It's a wonder they could unfold him at all after the delivery," she went on to joke. She reassured me that he was normal and wheeled me back to my berth. My husband arrived to find me in a much better state.

I stayed one day too long in the hospital. I had the Sunday turkey dinner twice. On day eight I was on my knees, in the hallway, begging my obstetrician, "Let me go home, please release me, let me go." He did. I think he was weary of me tugging on the hem of his lab coat as I tearfully followed him around. Whatever the deciding factor, I was a free woman, free to take home that tiny scrap of humanity for whom I was one thousand percent responsible. Now I was really scared.

I was not the same person. Little things confounded and bewildered me as never before. The line had been crossed. I had now entered parent world and there was no going back.

An example of how truly helpless I felt was my first attempt at airing the darling babe. I bravely unfolded the shining new carriage, gently placed said infant inside, and pushed. The beastly contraption would only turn endlessly in circles. I could only push and weep, following helplessly behind. My neighbour Daphne kindly came to my rescue and said, "It's the brakes. One wheel is locked and making it go in circles."

Life continued quite peacefully for a few weeks as Matthew and I came to grips with the reality of each other. I was tired, cranky, and crying continually. So was he. Yet I was gaining confidence, as I tentatively felt my way into my new life. With imperceptible momentum, I was becoming maternal, slowly falling head over slippers for the fruit of my womb. Can anyone ever verbalize the effect pregnancy, childbirth and caring for an infant has on your life, your being, on your very soul? This new state was draining away my selfishness. No longer was I a single unit; I had morphed into a celestial body with a diaper-clad moon orbiting my girth. Now my son's needs came first. His immediate physical demands were exhausting and labour intensive. Who knew? Who could have told me? I certainly would not have listened.

While lying in bed early one morning, I was sluggishly dragged to a semi-conscious state. An eerie, pitiful wail reached my ears. As I struggled from vegetable to animal, I focused on the source of the strange cry. The baby was whining, sort of. My mothering instincts kicked in. I tore loose from my cocoon of blankets and tumbled headlong into the nursery. A whimper of deafening quiet emanated from this helpless creature so entwined with my being that I vibrated to his plaintive call.

I immediately jabbed Matthew with the basal thermometre. He was a tiny human inferno. His temperature could not possibly be this high, 104° F. He blasted me with his body heat. I was terrified and bewildered. After I had called my husband to pick us up and given the baby a pain reliever, I waited by the front door, rocking both of us mindlessly.

I had been to the hospital emergency ward with Matthew just three days previously, that visit induced by a mild sunburn and low-grade fever. Ever cautious and vigilant, the ER staff had run thorough tests, including a urine culture, and done a routine physical exam. In the previous seventy-two hours there had been sufficient time for the culture to grow, so it was only a matter of minutes after our second arrival that a doctor told us, "He has a urinary tract infection, we're keeping him in."

We weren't going anywhere fast. I prepared to settle in for a week or so. My son was very sick. Only later would I learn how deathly ill he was and how perilously close we had come to losing him.

Since it was still quite early in the day and the discharges had yet to leave, we were stuck in the ER for the duration. It would be a very long wait. Michael kissed me and departed, with relief I'm sure, for a very important business lunch. Would I even have lunch? My vision of being Madonna with child was fading rapidly. Closer to reality was an overweight hausfrau tenderly clutching her waif in a bundle of bunting bag.

At this point, a nurse gently removed my baby from my tenacious grasp to administer a spinal tap. This is not an easy, painless test, nor is it a short test. It consisted of piercing his tiny six-week-old spine with a huge needle and removing fluid. I cringed listening to his screams from across the hall. I was prohibited from being present and the procedure lasted for two agonizing hours. That was the first time I cried. The passage of over twenty years has done nothing to dim the memory of how we both suffered that day in 1985.

Finally, I retrieved my baby. He was limp with exhaustion, weary of doing battle with the uniformed medical personnel. I requested and was placed in an examining room alone so I could nurse Matthew, to calm him as well as myself. The nurse attending him had inserted an intravenous drip into his head. This unusual site had been chosen since an infant's veins are so minute that they are impossible to locate, except for the larger, more developed veins in the head.

We were both enjoying our respite from the hospital's continual intrusion, when I noticed Matthew's skull was quickly swelling. The fluid being pumped into him was not being delivered, but was pooling under his scalp. In my panic I had no way of alerting a nurse, or so it seemed. I stared hopelessly at the closed door with my breast locked in the maw of my contented, suckling son. I resisted raising the alarm, so as not to frighten Matthew, and thankfully a nurse came in at this crucial moment and rescued us. With a velvet touch that belongs only to nurses and angels, she removed the IV and in a kind gesture said, "Ask for Dominique when she gets on at seven. She can find a good vein in a haystack." This Florence Nightingale was reputedly incredible at finding veins on diminutive patients. This was a talent I was not familiar with, but I remain forever in her debt. She was the first nurse I encountered as I wandered upstairs and she was able to place the needle in the right spot, so right that they used it for the entire stay. Frequently, an artery collapses and the exercise begins anew.

Somehow we survived in the emergency room all day. I did not eat anything and never went to the washroom. I was slightly delirious. Much, much later we were transferred upstairs: Matthew, his mommy and his gurney. How very tiny and forlorn a newborn looks laid out on a gurney. Matthew got the bed and I got a cot with a window view. Don't ever fool yourself into believing you can sleep in a hospital ward, not unless you are receiving some good drugs. As only the parent of the patient, I was not so lucky as to be entitled to medication. I dozed intermittently, worrying my thin covers into knots and tossing fitfully in my half-sleep. Early morning brought a new shift of nurses signing on and a dutiful husband with breakfast.

"It's Macdonald's," he said, gesturing towards the obvious golden arches. "I hope you can eat."

I've never found that to be a problem. How does one settle into a hospital ward? Where do I put the doilies? Actually, the rhythm of the routine was easy to assimilate. Soon, even the guards thought I was a nurse, what with my purposeful stride and my very visible presence.

I didn't know enough to know how bad things were. The doctors withheld this knowledge to protect us until after the crisis had passed and Matthew was stable. Even as fear gained a foothold, I still had an underlying sense of peace. Sunlight poured over my son's bed in a molten stream, seemingly direct from the great one Himself. I gazed at my tiny boy, the object of all my hopes, dreams and nightmares of late. He was almost too small to war-rant such an outpouring of energy. My "little boy blue," as his Nana called him, was so utterly beautiful, with quite white skin and full red lips. His dark hair glistened and radiated good health while all the tests indicated otherwise. He was active, aware and interested in his surroundings. How could he be so sick?

I went to the mall and purchased two items, a rectangular mirror approximately six inches long and a panda puppet. The black and white bear was supposed to be visually stimulating for a young baby, or so the popular theory went at the time. I was a new mother eager to provide for my child so he could go to college ten years early, and I bought it. The mirror proved to be the greatest toy. One of the nurses had suggested it as entertainment, not knowing my son's Zodiac sign was Leo. What do Leos love to do? Look at themselves, even at six weeks old. Matthew contentedly gazed at his reflection for hours. He still does to this day.

Matthew's father, Mike, was a much better mother than I was. He could take the squalling, wailing and screaming, though he suggested, "I should invent a sound proof helmet for babies."

I was terrible. When a baby cried, I really hated it. What did they want? Why wouldn't they stop? I got all nervous and panicky at the smallest cry. A knot formed in the pit of my stomach at the sign of a whimper. I always thought I wouldn't know what to do or that they were sick and would die. I knew it was pathetic and paranoid. Even the slightest cough caused me to worry.

For a man who didn't want a baby until he was sure where the relationship was going – and we were four years married already – Michael was a great dad. He bonded with our one-eyed jack – our nickname for Matthew, who could only keep one eye open at a time that first day – from the minute he laid eyes on him. The guy fell in love.

I became familiar with the flow of my world. I bobbed in the waves of the hospital's rigorous routine and tried to be normal. Planes crashed and people died on the outside. I knew nothing of that – I didn't read and I didn't hear. I became very isolated as I focused on my infant. He needed me to be near and to nurse him. He was everything now, the centre of my universe.

The Montreal Children's Hospital is a teaching hospital, so when a doctor inquired if his residents could see Matthew I wasn't surprised. What did startle me was the specific reason they chose him for inspection. These student doctors had never examined a healthy-looking baby before. Most babies in the hospital looked sick. This was an opportunity to poke, touch and basically handle an otherwise well infant with no obvious signs of infection or disease. The diverse crew of wanna-be physicians swarmed into our room following the leader like a school of fish. They were reticent at first but with encouragement soon began to ask questions of me and of their professor. Imagine, with only a few weeks' experience, I was actually the expert on my son. The students struck me as eager, intelligent and young, yet in a short while, they would be diagnosing and treating their own patients.

One young woman stood out. She placed herself physically apart from the group. Her lustrous, ebony mane rested veil-like on her slight shoulders and her head tilted to one side as if to catch all the words as they scurried by. She was the one who asked me, with the empathy that all great healers have, "How are you managing and coping with the unexpected strain of a hospital stay with a sick baby."

Still in shock, I told her, "It isn't easy but I really don't know anything yet. What exactly is a UTI? What does it mean for my son?" I didn't have any answers and I hardly even knew the questions.

His night nurse came on duty after completing reports and found me hovering over Matthew's bed with my chin quivering almost imperceptibly to the beat of some sad song. I felt forlorn and was having a seat on the pity pot. Worry had left me dazed and unsettled. This older woman, (from a twenty-six year old's perspective almost every one seems older), must have sensed my vulnerability. With wisdom and experience borne of years of nursing, she gently enfolded me in arms that could have flipped a Hummer. Her embrace protected my frailty and apparent weakness with a strength that passed directly to my soul.

Outwardly she was rather ordinary, with strands of grey appearing randomly, like weeds on a lawn of chestnut-tinted hair. A checked handkerchief was perfectly angled from a breast pocket of a sweetheart pink uniform. Her hose hugged baggy knees and swollen calves.

She pulled me to the corner of my haven and lowered me to a rocking chair I had pilfered from down the hall.

Rocking chairs were a hot commodity and I was going to get mine. While I gently rocked with my cushioned bottom nestled on the pillow, I listened to a fellow human share her experience and hope. She stole time from her schedule to warm me and lighten my load. All this for a stranger who happened to be in her ward that night. You can't tell me there is no higher power. I felt it then and I continue to feel it to this day.

My father, Roger, came to visit. My mother came to mourn. She had aged ten years since the last time I had seen her.

My mother, Irma, was born in Bavaria in Germany. She moved to Canada in 1951 at the age of eighteen. She had had a choice of the Australian or Canadian door at the immigration office and ended up on a boat in the North Atlantic and a new life, while inhabiting the creative mind of an artist. As a child I remember her dragging herself upstairs from the basement studio to cook supper for us, often burning the vegetables as a result of hurrying back downstairs to her work. My father would often tease her about the regularity with which she blackened the food, filled the kitchen with smoke and left the burners on as we assembled at the dinner table. My mother wore no makeup and wore work clothes befitting her life in the country. She was short, well groomed and loved to wear comfortable shoes. She had always reminded me of Queen Elizabeth living in a log cabin.

My mother burst into the room wearing an anguished look that told of her fears for her only grandchild. She hugged me, which was unusual, and went to stand by

Matthew's crib near the window. She gazed at my son with such pain that I realized with a jolt that she suffered for me as well as the child. Her agony was palpable and seemed to form a miasma around her small form as she huddled in the dark, away from the light flowing in through the clear panes of the windows. My own misery abated as I assumed the mantle of caregiver for my mother. She needed to lean on me when I didn't feel capable of holding myself up. My mother stayed until she couldn't stay anymore.

The following day brought waves of sunshine from behind the lined hospital curtains. It seemed like a normal day. I slept in a cot like a soldier and felt like I had been in the trenches. My clothes and personal items were mashed in a sack at the foot of my rack. I was as rumpled as a bag lady and my grumpy demeanor poked its horny head out every time I muttered a word. The orderly filed in to take my baby for a series of chest X-rays. "Routine stuff," he informed me. "Nothing to worry about."

I got comfortable on a window seat near the nurses' station and called my husband at work. I was surprised when he seemed concerned about the procedure. I was naively unworried and remained so for a few hours until the results came back.

The words tumbled from the surgeon's lips and cascaded meaninglessly from his tongue to the floor. "There are some questionable spots on Matthew's lungs and we will have to investigate further. The very worst scenario would be cystic lung, a most unlikely diagnosis."

Did he say unlucky?

Michael was usually a calm man. In the ten years we had been together he had rarely raised his voice above dinner party conversation level, with his tone unchanging and his anger as slow to boil as a watched pot. His reaction to the news startled me. He totally freaked out. My husband paced with his arms tight at his side. His turmoil became evident as his steps pounded down ever harder and his face twisted into a contortionist's grimace. He was never the emotional type and the difficulty of suddenly dealing with an ocean of feelings was too much to contain. He continued his march and turned abruptly. Tears welled up in his hazel eyes and fell on his steel-toed boots. He clenched my shoulders in his lean, long fingers and pulled me to him. A button from his blue polyester work shirt pressed into my ear as Michael buried his face in my hair. His mask was gone; he was naked in his fear. I was stunned.

This display was beyond my imagination. Mike had always been the strong one, the defender of his numerous siblings. Due to his extraordinary height he had always been the one everyone relied on. Even at a young age he had had to fight the battles and act more grown up because he was taller and seemed older. Since childhood he had never spoken much, which added to the facade. I felt the steel stiffen in my spine as I realized that I could no longer be a woman-child in this marriage. I had to become a full partner and help elevate my spouse as we stumbled through this predicament.

2

SPOTTY LUNG

We soon had an answer to the mystery of the spotty lung. The worst-case scenario had become reality. The doctor attempted to explain the diagnosis and to prepare us for what was to follow.

Our son had an extremely rare congenital defect called cystic lung, which meant that he had pockets of air in his lung tissue. If left untreated or discovered too late, it would lead to infections and a collapsed lung. The prescribed treatment was a lobectomy, the surgical removal of my baby's lower left lung. Surgery is never performed on someone older than seven or eight, due to the lungs' inability to regenerate matter after that age. If the defect is discovered after that time, there is no medical recourse but to treat infections and possibly fatal collapses as they occur. They set the date for surgery seven weeks later, when the infection we were fighting now would be vanquished and my baby would once again be in good health, except for his sick lung.

Urinary tract infections are a rare condition for boys, almost exclusively affecting girls. Boys who are uncircumcised are almost four times more likely to need hospitalization for UTIs than those circumcised. The rate is lower than the twenty-fold risk previously thought and severe UTIs are relatively rare, making circumcision medically unnecessary.

Matthew's urinary tract infection was under control. The medicine being administered to my child was having an effect. He was healing. I, meanwhile, was clinging to my old life that was virtually dead. I was grasping at spirals of smoke, an illusion of Mom and Pop and that white picket fence.

With no other alternatives, I did what I had to, what I was told to and whatever I needed to. I weighed Matthew's diapers, washed and rocked him, and sang lullabies (very badly) to this helpless, tiny infant. As I breast fed Matthew I would imagine we were home. I wasn't really surrounded by harried nurses, beeping instruments and doctors' pagers, too-bright lights and a large contingent of sick kids. I was actually curled up on my plaid sofa with my baby's head cradled in the crook of my arm and Batman reruns on the television. Reality invariably came crashing back, like torrential rain through an open window in a hurricane. I wasn't home. I wasn't Dorothy, and this wasn't Kansas. Far from it. This wasn't even as good as the castle, with all those damn scary flying monkeys.

The next day unfolded with no inkling of the enormity of the challenge it contained. It began with another orderly advising me of more tests Matthew had to undergo. With Matthew's diagnosis of cystic lung, the prepatory work had begun for surgery the next month. On today's agenda was nuclear medicine.

The orderly loomed over me, hawk-like. His uniform gripped him tight under the arms only to fall away loosely at the waist. A revealing glimpse of hairy ankles in the gaps between cuffs and slouched socks completed the picture.

"They're going to do the work at the Royal Vic since the Children's doesn't have the facilities for this kinda test. Do you want to have a nurse escort?" he asked.

"No thanks, I'll be fine."

That was the wrong answer.

Matthew and I boarded an ambulance for the ride over. What a rush to be outside. The sky was an endless, cloudless blue. I gaped through the open window of the ambulance, anxious to savour and store for future enjoyment every assault on my previously hibernating senses. The air was pungent with smells, sweet to a nose exposed exclusively to hospital odours and cleaning agents. In order to travel, the nurse had removed the IV line, but left the needle in the site. It was a good vein that they wanted to preserve, so Heparin was injected to thin the blood and prevent coagulation until the drip could be resumed upon our return. I was under the misguided impression that the nuclear medicine exam was a simple procedure and would soon be completed. Thus I had only one spare diaper, no money and no clue.

The Royal Victoria Hospital sat on the mountain in the centre of Montreal. Its turreted silhouette cast a shadow upon meticulously manicured lawns that welcomed visitors and patients. As we turned yet another corner up the curved drive, my attention was drawn to a door that looked better suited to a thatched cottage in rural England. It was partially hidden by an overgrown wild rosebush with a full complement of tiny yellow roses weighing down the spindly branches. The driver slammed to a stop in front of the portal that seemed so oddly incongruous with the modern world. This was my stop. My sweaty thigh was pinched painfully as the vinyl bucket seat refused to give up its grip on my posterior during my comical and unflattering descent to the pavement. Rubbing my leg vigorously to alleviate the sting, I haltingly made my way through the door. I had entered another dimension.

The futuristic room was in complete juxtaposition to the old-world exterior of the building. I felt like I was striding onto the deck of the Starship Enterprise. Hi-tech machines were strewn about the massive, sparsely furnished room. They were placed in some unknown alien pattern, like spokes jutting out from a giant hub. My eyes fell on the fascinating centrepiece. It gleamed eerily as it winked and blinked to greet me. Trembling, I stood and waited with Matthew, asleep in his car seat on the linoleum floor. The attendant hustled out of his cubicle. He was extremely white. Both his immaculate uniform and alabaster skin gleamed in the dim electronic light. His long arms with similarly tapered fingers reached down to retrieve my papoose. With silent movements and whispered commands he ushered me into the preparation room. I fell into a chair. Matthew was placed on a gurney, raised high in the eye of the storm, as nurses and technicians swirled around his tiny form. The first problem they encountered was the lack of an adequately small oxygen mask to fit over his face. They needed to pump radioactive gas into his tiny lungs and were unprepared for a baby. This was a hospital equipped for adults, a difficulty that would be a recurring theme throughout the rest of the day.

Once the gas was administered – aided by Matthew's screaming, which, I'm sure, sucked the stuff further into his lungs – we marched into the adjoining room. Matthew was placed on some sort of tray in front of the big machine – a sacrificial altar to the god of science-fiction, perhaps? With a flick of the attendant's skinny fingers the equipment hummed into action and a transmission from Matthew's airways leapt onto the screen. Sparkles danced and blazed above me in the darkened room. It was a light show, a fireworks display. It couldn't be my son's lungs, giving a reading of who knows what. My instructions followed. I was to hold down the frightened baby, to keep him completely still for a hundred second intervals, seven times. Even one time seemed impossible. My task became a labour of Herculean proportions that consumed the entire day and all of my energy.

With no one to care for me, I neglected myself by forgetting to eat or rest. There seemed to be no opportunity to take a break. I was not thinking rationally. For example, even when I really had to pee, I was convinced nobody else could mind the baby. The nurse escort I had so ignorantly refused earlier would have been a good thing. I had to be with Matthew every minute, including the minutes necessary for bodily functions. I hauled Matthew into the bathroom with me and with the dexterity of a juggler, I managed to lower my trousers, underwear and derriere, place the baby prone across my legs, and finally relieve myself. I was consumed with self-pity. I was ravenous, exhausted and post-partum, with an infant on my lap, while I urinated. I was the helpless one. My head dropped to my chest as I fought back the flood of tears pooled just behind my eyeballs. My resistance diminished and the walls of strength and denial I had so carefully constructed came crashing down and I began to weep. Softly at first, the trickle became a stream, as great sobbing wails shook the walls of the washroom, a slightly incongruous place for my breakdown. Matthew, startled, joined in the chorus. A pounding on the stall brought me back with a jolt as a kind voice offered assistance from the other side of the door.

"Do you need some help?"

It may as well have come from the other side of the world. The entire experience was surreal. I was alone and very afraid to go on. But I had to pull up my pants and get out of the toilet.

Holding a baby still for a hundred consecutive seconds is not possible. It's like trying to hold a fish down as it flops around in the bottom of your boat after you've removed the hook. If Matthew moved even a fraction of an inch, the shot would be no good, and he moved a lot. As the day wore on, we all began to wear out. As my temper frayed and began to flare, I pushed myself to remain calm and to concentrate. I felt weak and wanted to lash out at someone, anything to feel powerful. With the grace of God and His impeccable timing, Matthew surrendered to sleep and the odds for successful shots swung in our favour. The technician almost clapped as he completed the first scan. He would want to dance a jig when they were all done. This had to be more grueling than working with animals on a movie set. A tiger or a poodle would have been more co-operative. The task of pinning him motionless consumed many punishing hours, but we did it.

I poured my aching body back into the ambulance. With Matthew secured in his infant seat, we began the journey home to the Montreal Children's Hospital, my sanctuary. It was late as we wended our way back down the mountain and ventured west. Oblivious to the fiery, reddening sky, I slumped wearily in my seat with my palms lifeless, face up, my eyes deadened and downcast. The sunset glowed so fiercely as to cause me to lift my heavy head. The radiance had painted the scenery and left flaming streaks everywhere. It was heavenly.

Michael came to visit after work only to find we had not returned from the Royal Vic. He rose to greet me with a curt hello and an impatient query about my day. Not waiting for a reply he retrieved Matthew from my grip and wandered, cooing softly, over to the window. I glanced at my husband as I lowered my weary self onto the makeshift bed. Somehow he appeared larger than life with his infant son cradled firmly on his forearm. Matthew's head was in Mike's oversized mitts and his feet wedged in the crook of Mike's elbow. I drank in the sweetness of his love and basked in the display of tenderness being shown to our son. This side of his personality had budded and bloomed with the birth. His new gentleness and displays of affection revealed feelings foreign to him just two months prior, and they were certainly surprising in their intensity. It amazed me that Michael was even capable of such behavior. Mike never held me that way and he only accepted my hand if I forced it on him. He told me he loved me twice, both times over the phone, once while he was in Las Vegas and the other time from a ski slope in the Swiss Alps.

I met Mike in a bar. Actually it was a discotheque. The requisite disco ball hung shimmering and spinning centre court, while the bell-bottomed young people shook their booties below. I was a fresh-faced seventeen-year-old with long brown hair parted in the middle and a naiveté that revealed my youth and inexperience. My belly was flat, my waist could be circled with one arm and I loved to dance. I had borrowed my best friend Bev's boyfriend, Gary, for the evening and was sitting with him and his friend Alexandra, when I noticed a lanky stranger sauntering over to our table. He was tall, broad-shouldered, with a healthy mane of blond hair.

Alexandra claimed him as her boyfriend and wiggled over to make room for him to join us. Mike positioned himself directly opposite me and slouched into the booth. He wore a cowboy/pimp hat that shadowed his eyes and made it impossible to guess what he was thinking. He was unreadable, imposing, gorgeous and cool. I danced with some other guy I knew but could only imagine it was Mike pulling me close for the slow dance. Under the lowered lashes of my pretend-closed eyes, I watched Mike watching every turn I made on the floor.

Alexandra must have noticed, because within minutes she hissed a warning. "Keep your hands off of my man."

I didn't. Through Gary I slipped him my number and was rewarded with a phone call the next day. It didn't seem soon enough.

It was snowing lightly outside my window as I stretched out on my bed and talked for almost two hours to the handsome man of my dreams. We arranged to meet at Bev's father's camera store the following evening before going bowling and I got the shock of my life when he strode into the building. He had to duck to get through the door. With his cowboy boots and hat, he seemed seven feet tall. I turned to Bev and nervously exclaimed, "What have I got myself into?"

I can still remember our first kiss. Mike, so long and slim, leaned over me by the pinball machine in the arcade and set off all my bells and whistles. I had swooned in his arms. I was hooked.

Back on the ward, I was startled out of slumber. I groggily realized that it wasn't time for recess as I had been dreaming, but that some alarm or something had sounded. It turned out to be the monitor for the IV drip of the child in the next bed. It would have to be reset by a nurse. I relaxed slightly and yearned for my bed. My queen-size, four-post brass bed, with its majestic, sleep-inducing mattress and thick, extra goose down stuffing in a cloud-like duvet that awaited me in my bedroom. So unlike my present surroundings: the peeling yellow paint, the dust bunnies in the corners and behind the dressers, the non-stop intrusions on time and mind, the utter lack of privacy. The situation was beginning to grind me down.

Fortunately, the week of recovery was coming to a close. Matthew's health was almost completely restored and all that remained was to set the date for surgery. Dr. Laberge made a pit stop in our room, his schedule so crammed with operations and emergency room work as to preclude a lengthier visit. He explained that the nuclear tests had shown it was cystic lung. He went on to tell me how, with a rib spreader, he would open the chest cavity and remove the lower left lobe.

"With a patient so young, the tissue will regenerate and fill the lung cavity. I've cleared my calendar for the morning of November 27, since I don't want to delay the operation any more than is necessary."

The effects of Matthew's near fatal infection would completely dissipate within the six-week, pre-op time frame. I was left stunned and unsure of how to tell Mike the news.

I prepared to leave the hospital with mixed emotions. Yes, I was ecstatic to be returning home to immerse myself in my own environment and yet I was strangely wistful about leaving the security and care provided by the hospital. This whole mother thing was dreadfully hard and I was hesitant to continue alone.

I tried to settle into my old life but it was as if I had grown several sizes and none of my clothes fit. Nothing seemed familiar. I was struggling to adapt to Matthew's rhythms and go with a flow that had no rhyme or reason. I had always been very structured and organized. Forget that. Babies, or at least my baby, didn't seem to do what I wanted when I wanted it. Fatigue dragged me down. Sleep was reduced to snatching a couple of hours between night feedings. I continued to breast feed since I believed in its inherent health benefits and because I felt it was all I could do as a mother to make him well. Only the doctors and the nurses had the power to cure him.

It was our fourth wedding anniversary and I wanted lobster. I really wasn't in any state to go out so we decided to stay home in our little apartment and celebrate in the tiny eat-in kitchen. My crustacean craving was satisfied by two of the tasty critters, delivered by Mike after work along with champagne, my other favourite delight. I set the mood with candles casting a romantic light on the antique oak table and the good china displayed on Irish linen. Mike arrived, bearing my dinner order and hurried into the shower. I contentedly worked at creating a gastronomic delight while humming the theme from Winnie-the-Pooh and anticipating the evening's entertainment. I was living in fantasyland, dreaming in Technicolor. I was still quite bulky from the pregnancy and was imagining a slim sexy me sitting down to a fantastic feast, replete with wine, that would satisfy all my desires. I plunked myself into my seat and looked at the baby in his swing next to the table. The reality didn't mesh with my cozy picture of connubial bliss.

We decided to attempt another enchanted evening the following night by planning an excursion to a fine dining establishment downtown. I squeezed my corpulent body into an unforgiving black taffeta gown, my voluptuous curves accented by the strained pulls at the zipper and seams. I piled my mahogany tresses in countless ringlets high atop my rounded visage and surveyed the results of my careful preparations. Maybe I was being overly critical, but there's only so much that can be accomplished with artful application of makeup and queen-size, control-top pantyhose. I tearfully made my way to the front room where my patient husband stood waiting. Bless him. He told me, "You're gorgeous and I would marry you all over again."

We bundled up Matthew and deposited him with our friends, Gary and Rosario, who were expecting their first child in February and wanted a practice baby. They were delighted to be entrusted with our son for our first date. We left them with prepared formula, diapers, a complete wardrobe – just in case – and every other baby essential and non-essential that existed in 1985.

We were euphoric as we headed downtown to the restaurant. We wanted our night to be a celebration of life, our new son's as well as, hopefully, our resuming one. The restaurant came highly recommended, with many accolades from our friends and food critics alike. We were aware of the elegant ambiance the minute we entered the place, the scent of luxury wafting even to the massive carved door. Cloistered dining areas ensured intimacy and privacy for the obviously well-heeled clientele. I decided not to think about the price of the meal.

We crossed the restaurant on a carpet with pile so dense that I feared being swallowed as we were ushered to a booth tucked away in a dimly lit corner. It was perfect. Candlelight was my best defense. I wanted to be beautiful and desirable. I was super sensitive, highly aware of my zaftig figure, and was my own harshest judge. It would be impossible to be his dream girl again if I continued to reproach myself for not having lost all the weight yet. My body would eventually yield to diet and exercise, once Matthew was out of danger and fully recovered from the surgery. I couldn't even begin to wrestle with this issue in my present mindset and emotional turmoil. A whiff of garlic and roasted meat drifted by our table, causing me to cast aside all thought of scales and celery sticks. Dinner was the definition of ambrosia. When I asked him how he liked it, Michael answered that it was "alright." Not easily impressed, he must have enjoyed something, because he left a generous tip.

Satiated, I relaxed into the seat of the car to savour the return journey. I was downright giddy with the sense of freedom I was enjoying without the baby. It was incredible to be so selfish and think only of myself for three hours. My fantasy metre had expired, though, and it was time to collect the child. Rosario was impressed with both of them. "He was such a good baby. He drank the entire bottle in no time at all."

Inexperience turned off the alarm that should have sounded over this feeding frenzy. He should have been gradually introduced to formula and not taken in copious quantities all at once. I was unaware of the trouble to come. I ignorantly waved good-bye and returned my tiny tot to the nest.

Normally, one should be grateful for small blessings. Changing fewer pooey diapers is a good thing. When this state of affairs continued for days and became no pooey diapers at all, I had cause for concern. We took

Matthew to Vermont for the weekend. My in-laws had a beautiful second home in the northernmost corner of the state, approximately ninety minutes from our house in a bedroom community of Montreal. We spent most weekends and holidays there with Mike's parents, Jackie and John, as well as Mike's siblings, their respective spouses and assorted friends. The place was a sprawling spread that could sleep twenty people comfortably, had two kitchens, two living rooms, two saunas, a Jacuzzi, and a "passion pit." This little nook above the main kitchen was actually a queen size bed built into a corner with three walls and paisley curtains to close it off. Adjacent to the passion pit was a fireplace, and surrounding this was yet another den. The property also sported a tennis court and a built-in pool that had served me well during my pregnancy, except for all the skinny young things that would sunbathe around it making me appear all the more rotund.

Matthew's clogged drainage system was quite worrying to me and I tried assorted means to alleviate the problem. Prune juice in his baby bottle was the first method of my madness, followed by doses of mineral oil. Baby suppositories would be my final step. Nothing was working. I was becoming desperate. Imagine how Matthew felt.

Relief came swiftly and unexpectedly. I had Matthew in the kitchen and was giving him his lunch (left breast to be followed by right breast) when he suddenly exploded during his burp. I figured he just couldn't swallow one more drop. He was literally covered from head to toe in feces. I was stunned for about ten seconds and then started yelling for help, stripping the little tyke down to his filthy birthday suit. He was astonished as well and didn't even protest or move about. Perhaps he was overpowered by the stench. He clung to me while I lowered him into the bathtub for a scrubbing and he began to wail as the soap and water did their job. Once everyone's tears had dried, we were all in clean clothes and the crappy outfit had been tossed. Matthew and I settled down to finish lunch. I was sure he'd have more of an appetite now that this had been cleared up. He finished his meal and swiftly succumbed to sleep after a second, less eventful burp.

Monday morning Matthew had an appointment at the hospital with a renal specialist, Dr. Pianosi. I was nervous and uncertain about the visit. The state of my baby's kidneys was to be examined and if there was residual damage it could mean kidney failure. I glanced out the apartment window and stopped cold. A somber grey pall hung over the glistening oak out back. The electrical and telephone wires, coated in ice, drooped perilously close to the stiff needles of frozen grass below. While my artistic side reflected on the glittering natural beauty of the ice storm, my practical nature recoiled from the danger involved in maneuvering through freezing rain on roads slicker than a greased watermelon. I grabbed Matthew and stuffed him into his snowsuit. He protested with flailing limbs, a rebellious yowl and crocodile tears.

Great gusts of icy rain whipped over and around me as I tentatively made my way outside. All my strategic plotting could not keep me from slipping and sliding down the driveway that lay treacherously like a skating rink between my car and me. Fear gripped me with frozen tentacles and I prayed furiously to be somehow transported to the hospital safely. I glided, snowboarder fashion, down the incline, plunked Matthew in his car seat and emerged to tackle the elements. Sleet slashed at my cheeks as I futilely chiseled away the accumulated crust on the windshield. Unyielding ice resisted my hammering and scraping. My efforts paid off as the coating finally relented after many tears, countless curses and after the car's defroster was turned on.

Once on the road it got worse. Now the problem was the congestion on every major artery and alternate routes that were closed or impassable. My speed was so reduced (when I actually moved) as to be unreadable. I checked out the other drivers, bit players in my drama, and found their faces to be strained almost to cracking. My nerves were taut, growing ever more strained, as adrenaline overcame me with its intensity.

My sweet, sweet son was caterwauling in the back seat. He was placed facing rear as the law required and was tired of staring at fake leather. I grew edgier as his vocals escalated and tried humming a little Black Sabbath to tune him out. I pumped up the volume on the radio and drowned his cries but the echo of his wails ricocheted inside my head unceasingly like an India rubber ball. An eternity later, my car, knowing the trouble I have with parallel parking, turned on its autopilot, headed in the direction of a parking spot and slid sideways into perfect position. The fifty feet to the front door were pure ice with an uphill grade. This treacherous path was the final leg of my nearly impossible journey and I would make it if I had to crawl. I almost did. The salt spreader guy was obviously late for work, and I had to creep with miniscule steps along the edge of the building for support, clutching Matthew to my bosom to keep the panic at bay. I needn't have worried about being late. We were the only patients who made it in that morning. We were hailed as conquering explorers, intrepid vanquishers of the fierce, killer conditions that had prevailed and kept all others from their appointments. I didn't really want this much attention. Just poke him, test him and let us go.

We squeezed into a hole in the wall that had the requisite peeling paint and reeked of ammonia. I felt too large and quite ineffectual. Matthew wasn't feeling much of anything, but was dozing peacefully. The nurse wanted to put a catheter into my baby's penis. Talk about suffering indignities. I peeled away his furry blue bunting bag emblazoned with a little teddy flying a kite under a pointy golden sun, stripped his sleeper and lowered his onesies. When he was laid bare, she pushed the offending equipment up his private part and a few drops of blood trickled out. They were whisked away like dust on a computer screen and my son began to howl. He underwent an Intravenous Pyelogram, which tested kidney function, and a VCUG, which tested if the urine was flowing the right way without refluxing, and to see if there were any obstructions. I suffered silently for my baby. He had physical pain, but I was aware of feeling a deeper, emotional malaise, far more powerful. It went to my very core. I had been unable to protect my baby. This intrusion, and other assaults to his little body, were the consequences.

The roads had been cleared of ice by the salt trucks for the journey home. Matthew slept the sleep of the innocent the entire way. I began to prepare for the operation that lay ahead.

3

THE OPERATION

The appointed hour did arrive. We were asked to check in the Monday night before the Wednesday surgery to allow for a full day of pre-op stuff – needles and things. Packing for a hospital stay is not like going to Florida. Besides not needing a bikini, one doesn't even require shoes, slippers being the only footwear necessary. I left the designer dresses and brought sweat pants, jeans and T-shirts. I was going to be comfortable no matter what.

Tuesday dawned clear and cold. My mind cranked open its shutters to reveal fuzzy, matted thoughts. My body was hot. I felt as if my skin was ready to crack. I was powerless over my environment and I was already feeling gritty and uncomfortable. This did not bode well for the days ahead.

The surgeon fairly bounced into my quarters in the morning to give me the pep talk. Dr. Laberge started with, "Things should go well, it's a fairly cut and dried procedure."

I paid close attention while he continued with more information about the operation and recovery. He droned on, while my thoughts wandered to what colour tie the good doctor would sport the next day. I really didn't want to be there.

"Could you wear a red tie during surgery, for good luck?" I interjected. Dr. Laberge smiled, understanding that fear led me to ask for such an inconsequential favour.

"Sure."

Colour scheme decided upon, he bade me well and departed until the morrow.

My attention wandered to the only other occupants of the ward. A young mother was adjusting the blanket in her child's crib, her attempt at normalcy in the midst of change and the unknown. I ventured over to introduce myself and practically fell down at the sight of the young girl in the bed. She was no more than three years old and when she turned her head towards me, she revealed a monstrous deformity that left me quite unhinged. Cowardly as I felt, I was not cruel, nor was I unkind, so I continued to make my way over to stand beside the mother and her unfortunate progeny. After brief introductions, the mother, barely out of her teens, was quite forthcoming on her daughter's condition and prognosis.

"Maryanne needs many plastic surgeries to have somewhat normal features, normal enough that people won't stare at the sight of her," she explained. I hadn't been very discreet. She had noticed.

While I was so near Maryanne, I openly studied her condition. The right side of her face was like a werewolf's. It was covered in coarse brown and grey hair that sprung up from skin with a darker pigmentation than the rest of her body that was otherwise unaffected. After viewing her for a length of time, I actually stopped noticing the patch that extended from above her eyebrow to the curve of her chin. With nothing else to do we became friendly and spent most of that day, and the days following, together.

Sally was quite spirited, an independent woman who was generous and giving. When I admired a colourful stuffed bird hanging from a thin nylon wire near the bedside, she went out and bought one exactly like it for Matthew. It perched for the next week on the iron railing of his bed, calling out to all visitors with its brilliant plumage and a horrendous squawk each time it was knocked or fondled. His toy bird lost its caw many moons ago. To this day he lives sewn onto a pirate costume, to be trotted out on Halloween.

Pre-op was purgatory. There was a lot of waiting around to do and hell was the next stop. Matthew was removed for this test, wheeled away for that one, and I sat beside his empty bed knowing the next day would be worse. My anticipation began to build. The day wore on, eroding my strength as it bullied me with demands. I felt my will slowly dissipating, compelled to obey even the simplest request. It was easier than making a decision or even reasoning. Ground down like grist in a mill, my kernel of self, my defining quality, was fast disappearing. Too weak of spirit to fight, I struggled alone to cope with the pressure.

My husband was working late and passed by much later to tuck us in. Michael poked his head around the corner and flashed a big grin. That alone was suspect, as Mike seldom smiled – I only have two pictures out of hundreds that actually show his teeth. It occurred to me that perhaps he was scared stiff and was trying to cover up his feelings. This was just a guess, as Mike rarely shared his emotions with me. The closest he ever came to revealing bits of himself were at Matthew's birth and his grandfather's death. That was when his feelings had been too close to the surface and his emotions too raw to keep under wraps – he had exposed himself. Both times he had recovered quickly, so no one could ever see what lay beneath his exterior. Why did he need to protect himself from me, I wondered.

Mike tried to tell a dirty joke. I didn't get it. We sat dumbly across the bed from each other, our child an island between us, as we fumbled to express ourselves. We each failed for different reasons. I failed because I sensed Mike didn't want to hear how I felt or what I was thinking. Michael failed because he couldn't deal with my pain; he could barely begin to bear his own.

Michael drifted away home and I was alone. Matthew would begin fasting at midnight. I could give him a last feeding just before and then nothing by mouth after that. I yawned and stretched my aching limbs, numb after hours of unaccustomed inactivity. Reaching into the crib, I clasped my tiny babe to my breast and slid silently to a rocking chair with as much excess padding and stuffing as I had. I slid my feet as I always did when too weary, sick or tired to lift them – the extra effort of raising my knees might put me over the edge.

As I settled into the armchair, a coil poked me in the keister and it took some readjusting to outmaneuver it. Finally, nestled on one side, I took a moment to register my surroundings. Matthew was sleeping deeply, I was loathe to wake him. With the late hour had come some semblance of peace, or at least the hospital version of quiet. Most monitors were on low, most visitors had departed and the lights dimmed. I gently woke my son so that he could suckle and I allowed my head to fall back while he nursed. His pull was strong and the vacuum seal around my nipple was impenetrable. He would need every ounce of energy I could give him for the operation and recovery to follow. Given a good twenty minutes per side, his hunger subsided and he relaxed into my warmth, satiated. I cuddled him and pondered the situation.

I could hail a taxi and take him home so that they wouldn't need that rib spreader tomorrow. Tears of dread escaped and wandered down my cheeks. How could I just hand over my baby? Maybe they had made a mistake and there was nothing wrong?

I clutched Matthew desperately to my chest, placed his tiny face on my shoulder and rocked rhythmically, wishing it was all a bad dream. The nightmare continued and I reluctantly put him back to bed.

The next day dawned, of course. What did I think? The inevitable was happening, the operation would proceed. Wiping the sleep from my eyes, I stumbled down to the bowels of the hospital to search for the parents' showers. Their whereabouts were a mystery to me and top-secret for everyone else, but with my unerring sense of direction I finally located them. With trepidation I entered the washroom, nervously selected a stall, and pulled back the cheap cream-coloured plastic curtain to reveal sparkling white tiles. My worry about catching God-knows-what from God-knows-who vanished. I gingerly adjusted the spray to just below lobster and stepped in to enjoy the experience. If my voice had been a little better than a croak I would have sung a song. I was that happy to be alive.

Basically, I am an optimist with a *joie de vivre* that cannot be contained by external forces or by others' unrealistic limitations and restrictions on me. I have never really given much heed to what people thought of me and cared even less as I got older.. So a simple soak in the shower could refresh me and revive my spirits sufficiently to tackle another day.

Shampooed, soaped, ears swiped, teeth brushed and wearing clean undies (in case I was in a car accident), I made my way back upstairs to face the dragon. I hurried the final few feet and arrived just ahead of the crowd. Mike, preoccupied with his own very private thoughts, embraced me and turned to our baby. His shoulders sagged, unable to support the weight of his heavy head that hung low in despair. Waves of sadness emanated from this wonderful, difficult, troubled man.

The surgeon entered and proudly flashed his red tie. That gesture certainly portended good fortune. Things would go well, I thought. Yet as quickly as my spirits were raised, my hopes could be dashed again, by nothing more significant than a raised eyebrow or a misguided comment. I was in a sea of worry, lost without a life-jacket and with no sign of land. Spiritually bereft, I struggled alone with my fears for my baby's life.

Things began to happen quickly. I had little opportunity to cuddle Matthew as he was suddenly rolled away to the operating room. He left two worried parents in his wake.

"He must be starving," I said to no one in particular.

My stunned husband nodded bleakly, not budging, just staring at the door through which our son had just disappeared. I slumped into my seat as the uncertainty of the situation dawned on me. Though the risk of death was small, it was real, too real for me to handle at the moment. Sitting around was not the answer. I needed to do something. My husband was as lost as I was, so I grabbed his limp hands and hauled him out of the hospital.

After donning the paraphernalia necessary for an excursion in the Montreal winter, we scrambled out the revolving doors. Shocked by an icy gust of wind, we stood gaping like a couple of goofs. Buffeted by the continuous blasts of Canadian cold, we decided to seek shelter, away from the pressure of the hospital. Alexis Nihon Plaza was directly across the park from where we trembled and shivered. We ran down the gravel path, disregarding the traffic and the lights, and plunged headlong towards the mall. We arrived safely as fools and innocents always do. No injury could befall me when my entire focus was on my baby's survival, or so I reasoned.

Mike pulled the heavy glass door open and I slid in ahead of him. I followed the checker board pattern on the floor. Black, white, black, white, the squares led me to the main atrium in centre court. Palm fronds extended upwards. Columns covered with miniscule tiles formed intricate patterns, the result of some artisan's months of delicate labour, for the delight of a few observant souls. I collapsed on a stone bench, landing with a crunch and bruising my tailbone. What does one do when their child is under the knife? I had no precedent, no guidelines to follow. Mike didn't seem to have a clue.

The aroma of coffee drifted by my nostrils, luring me to the food court. Maybe this would help pass the time. Putting one foot in front of the other was a supreme effort. Every step took a conscious thought to execute, but slowly I managed to get to the café. I grasped the counter for support and swayed as if on the deck of a seafaring ship. Almost nauseous, I realized I would probably gag if I so much as took a sip of the brew. Shaking and sputtering, I meandered back to my bench. My bewildered spouse followed mutely.

The office tower above us released its hungry hordes for lunch. The crowds dipped and surged around us. I was blind, deaf and dumb. From somewhere deep in my core a little voice chimed in. Feed me.

When had I eaten last? It felt like acid had burned away my insides and I was just a shell, a casing, with nothing but fire in my gut. Trembling, I once again headed off on a mission with my life partner trailing behind.

I approached the Lebanese food kiosk with trepidation. Forcing myself to stand in line, I grew more sickened as I drew nearer to the cash. The attendant continued to belt the register as I gave him my order. He didn't seem to notice that I was an emotional basket case. He would notice if I didn't pay him though, so I handed over my money and grabbed a tray. With my plate heaped with steaming falafel in pita and a double portion of parsley salad, I wandered between the melamine tables bolted to the floor. I searched for a place to lay down my load. Giving up the hunt, I hiked my bulk up to a window ledge and balanced my food on my knees.

Who was I kidding? I could no more eat now than do six cartwheels while whistling Dixie. In disgust, I ditched the chow and leaned heavily into the corner of the hallway, an unexpected haven. Slave to my fears, my body was out of my control. I could will myself to eat but I could not put the fork to my mouth nor make my tongue push the food in once it passed my lips. I tried to think positively. A little bit of starving would probably be good. My body could feed on the stored up fat.

Mike wandered away. As I ran to catch up, I grabbed at his coat. My fingers felt so tense that they were almost brittle. My knees buckled. With my last drop of energy, I staggered back to my sturdy bench and weakly surrendered to my overwhelming sense of hopelessness. I felt unable to cope with anything. All around me people carried on as if nothing was happening, while my life was falling apart.

The passing of time registered somewhere in the outer periphery of my radar. I looked up at the clock suspended in the centre of the plaza near the escalator. With a mixture of relief and dread, I realized we had to go back to surgery for news of Matthew's condition. I practically pushed Mike along in my eagerness to return to the hospital. Suddenly I was flooded with strength, possibly an adrenaline rush.

I burst into the Intensive Care Unit and heard a baby cry. Following my maternal instinct, I turned in the direction of the sound. A nurse who spotted me asked, "Who are you? May I help you?"

How dare she accost me. Didn't she know that was my baby crying?

"My son, Matthew, is out of surgery. He was just crying."

While she searched for the location of his bed, I barged into a tiny room, certain my son needed me. There lay my tiny angel. I was ushered out just as quickly by the head nurse – they weren't ready for me yet. But I had seen him. He was alive and seemed okay. I could wait another hour, maybe.

Elated, I went for a cup of coffee with Mike. It was weak and bitter, quite a combination to pull off. My mind was on the ninth floor, in the C-wing with Matthew, reviewing the glimpse I had of him. My son looked like some mythical Greek monster with several wires and hoses extending from his body, hodge-podge, without symmetry. I was both apprehensive and joyful about being reunited with him. I waited on a cafeteria stool as sand drained through the hourglass.

Reality was greater than even my fertile imagination. Happiness flooded my senses when I was finally allowed to see Matthew. Tenderness for my first born filled me with grateful tears.

His size-small oxygen mask was steamy with vapour, as droplets formed above the hospital-issue soother he was sucking contentedly. He was also attached to a heart monitor, a pulse monitor, an IV, a lung drain and a stomach hose. I was informed that he would not need a transfusion as he had begun to produce enough blood to make up for the loss during surgery.

I stood dumbly adoring my baby, when my oft-forgotten husband nudged me further into the small isolation room. I beamed down on Matthew with every ounce of love I possessed, drinking in the beauty that was my son. He was heavily bandaged. His torso and left shoulder were wrapped in crisp white gauze. Specks of red stained the dressing like spilled wine. Matthew lay inert except for his rhythmic sucking. Funny, I had never seen a pacifier in his mouth; it looked stupid.

I was allowed to pick him up, but how? His collection of equipment was pure science fiction, and I needed an instruction manual to decipher exactly how to remove him from his bed. I inched closer to the tangle of infant and rubber. It seemed simple: bend over, retrieve patient. I was paralyzed with uncertainty. He seemed so helpless, so fragile. Would I hurt him? Would something fall off, like his head? Overcoming my fear, I simply went ahead and did it. I gently slid my hands under Matthew, raising him with a movement that was more of a caress than a lift, and lowered ourselves into a rocking chair. The rail along the bedside had been lowered to accommodate the short mess of wires that crept to the floor and wormed their way up to control central. I performed an intricate dance to arrange them in a pattern that would allow me to sit down without crushing the wires or Matthew.

Finally settled, I studied my son. His perfection at birth, marred only by the sudden appearance of a tiny mole between his left pinky and ring finger, was marred again by a tremendous cut that wound its way from his chest to beyond his shoulder blade. The scar would fade with time, but would I ever recover?

Matthew stirred. His opaque eyelids fluttered faintly, opening to reveal eyes the colour of stormy Caribbean waters. My little boy weakly turned to peer at me, a raspy squeak limply escaping from his parched throat. This is where I could have, should have, fallen apart. My reserves were greater than I had surmised, because now that the actual operation was completed and I was free to break down, I didn't. A young lady had woken up that morning, but she retired an adult. Something momentous had happened and it was so very painful.

There were no accommodations in intensive care hotel, so my hubby gathered me up and transported me home. This was definitely a good thing. The last hospital stay had been harder simply because I had stayed twenty-four hours a day. I had been deprived of news, stimulation, normal people, everyday activities and real air.

Following the surgery, we decided to go home every night around 11 p.m. and return by 6 a.m. the next day. I planned on continuing to breast-feed and I wanted to nurse Matthew as if we were at home. But we were not at home and wouldn't be for about ten days. The laundry pile grew dramatically that week, as I left it and every other chore untended. My husband probably began wearing his underwear inside out by day seven. I didn't ask. I didn't really care.

There was a hum in my brain that pushed me over the edge. I needed Mike's support to get to our apartment door and to jockey my way down the hall. Once beside my bed I dropped to the quilt, landing in a pretzel-like twist, because I had wanted to land on my back. Silly me. I felt quite worn out. I dropped into sleep, fully clothed, wearing my winter coat, hat and big old boots.

Before I even had a chance to rest it was morning. Not real morning, like for other people, but 5 a.m., when-everyone-else-is-still-in-bed morning. I stumbled out to the car, already dressed from the night before, after a quick swipe at my teeth with a toothbrush and a splash of water on my face. I waited in the car, warming it while my husband showered, shaved, got dressed and basically raced through his routine at a snail's pace. Why was he wasting my time? Didn't he realize I had to be at the hospital ten minutes ago? It was dark and gloomy before the dawn. I felt the same way.

I careened like a madwoman around the corners and through the hallways of the hospital, as my coat flapped a clear message of desperation. I seemed to know instinctively how to do crazy.

Mike gave up trying to follow and turned up later with doughnuts tucked under his arm like a football. I took a bite and, brushing icing sugar off my nose, I leaned forward. I expertly airlifted my son and with my help he executed a perfect landing on my plump lap. Sensing his hunger, I gingerly gripped him with one hand while unbuttoning my blouse. It had been less than twenty-four hours since the surgery. Could he possibly be ready to eat? Was he allowed to so soon? Not waiting for permission, I let nature take its course and supplied my baby with the nourishment he apparently needed. He latched on like a pro and in that special instant, I experienced an epiphany. After such a horrible day, I felt touched by an angel. We contentedly settled into our routine. Even now, my heart quickens with the memory of the feeling that overcame me for that one incredible moment.

Fatigue claimed me. My head suddenly weighed more than my neck could bear and dropped heavily to my chest. The chaos of the surgery and the trauma of the weeks leading up to it had passed. Having successfully scaled the peak, I was coming down the mountain. The exertion had depleted me of energy and I was floating somewhere above the dissipating storm clouds, all the while firmly grounded by Matthew's suction cup grip.

The serenity didn't last. Hot air seeped from my balloon. I unwillingly settled down to earth, overpowered by the reality of life after surgery. My weakness was compounded by lack of sleep and mounting fears of the unknown. Negatives hurtled themselves at me like a freight train bound to knock me over. Matthew was susceptible to infection and maybe his wound wouldn't heal. I could get sick and die, leaving him an almost-orphan. He could receive the wrong medication or a miscalculated dose. I was a willing martyr who dismissed the reassurances of the professionals and loved ones around me.

On the plus side, I knew babies and small children have the wonderful ability to recover quickly from trauma, unlike their adult counterparts who have grave anxieties and fears borne of life's experience. A child undergoing surgery doesn't stress over his mortgage, family, job or post-operative sex life. He engages life's mountains with the innocence of youth, protected by ignorance of his mortality and a natural optimism.

My parents appeared unbidden at my side. They were most welcome. I decompressed against my father's barrel chest. He held me up, my burning tears absorbed by his plaid shirt. I ventured a peek at my Dad and was astounded by my discovery. His eyes (surrounded by round cheeks and thick brows, encased in a jovial, bearded face) were moist to the point of being watery. This revelation bound me further to him as I clung childlike to his firm belly. He seemed an oasis of strength in my antiseptic world of efficient nurses, plastic pillows and anemic food. Guiltily, I recalled that my parents had lost their first baby, my brother. He had been extremely premature and had not survived. Maybe my dad was thinking about that little baby born so many years before, when my parents were barely out of their teens.

My father had been my employer until the day before Matthew's early birth and by working so closely together we had engendered an enduring, respectful relationship. After twelve years of making his coffee, typing his files and being his Girl Friday, I was adept at reading him. I was quite comfortable usurping his fortitude now when I so desperately needed it. My dad was consistent with his praise and his punishments in my so far, so-called great life.

I pulled away from his embrace to console my mom. She was a pitiful half-shell of a granny and surely could use some propping up. Her face hung with the weight of her worry; it seemed to sag in despair. She had always been an anxious, nervous type, and this medical emergency had pushed all her buttons. It wasn't her style to caress me. I told myself I didn't want it, or expect it, but I really could have used it. My mother tripped over this sort of raw, exposed emotion. Her family never displayed their soft underbelly, and the only feeling shown, albeit rarely, was anger.

I shared with my parents what I had gleaned so far from the medical professionals, who occasionally deigned to pause on their hurried routes to consult with us. Matthew wouldn't need a transfusion, the operation was considered a success, and he should be home in approximately ten days.

My parents hung around like last summer's sticky fly-paper, not really of much use. These two lovely people sensed when it was okay for them to return home, an hour commute from the hospital and light years away in stress and the reality of Matthew. I am sure they carried the worry with them in their anxiety bags. Matthew was their first grandchild and the time since his birth had been overwhelmingly difficult and full of unknowns. With their departure, I felt suddenly saddened and achingly adrift. My husband visited as much as possible, but it seemed his new business needed him more than I did. My tiny infant lay curled up in baby sleep. His softness spoke to me of gossamer and fairy wings, but my dreams for the future required major revision as every plan I had ever made lay in the ditch on the side of the road, covered in muck.

Not one to dwell on self-pity, I called on my resilience to drag myself away from daydreaming and deal with my duties. Now what exactly were they? Obviously I was to suckle the baby, but I wanted to know if I had any extra obligations. I cornered my nurse by the pharmacy, where I extracted the necessary information.

Christine was petite, with dark, glossy hair that she tied back to accentuate her high cheekbones. Her narrow hips were encased in dull beige cloth that failed to dim the luminosity of her skin. Her beauty made me uncomfortable in my own skin. She told me that Matthew's sponge bath, feeding and diapers were my domain and that every diaper had to be weighed and charted before and after it was used. Everything had to be recorded, all his input and output. Fancy that.

With renewed vitality, I returned to gaze at my near-perfect offspring. I relaxed into the rocking chair, and would have put my knees up to hug them if I had been less bulky. I settled for using a footstool to prop up my still-swollen feet and ankles and leaned my head and shoulders into the pillow. Finding and appreciating this rare moment of solitude, I continued to adore my son and restore my energy.

I must have dozed. In what seemed like just seconds later, I was jerked out of an almost drugged coma to confront a tearful, complaining baby. Christine was going off duty and wanted to take some measurements, including his temperature. This entailed the doffing of diapers and entry of the dreaded thermometre. It was not something that can be done to a sleeping patient and she had woken us both up in the process.

As she checked the reading, I noticed the graceful way she tended to Matthew. Her training and experience were evident as she maneuvered my son carefully to minimize his discomfort. She dipped her head as she lowered Matthew onto the bed and I wondered at her ability to accomplish so much with so little apparent effort and in such an efficient manner. Christine slipped away to reappear another day.

My baby was awake, so I tried feeding him. Since the surgery we had no schedule whatsoever and I hoped a regime would keep me sane. Matthew nuzzled my breast and quickly latched on. The pull of the rhythmic sucking seemed to extend all the way to my toes. The world has to stop revolving while you are both so pleasurably and intimately connected. Breast-feeding forced me to focus on Matthew and drink in his exhilarating, ethereal beauty. I inhaled and exhaled deeply, almost seeing stars from breathing in too much oxygen. I felt the tension ebb from my atrophying muscles, as the collective strains of the past few weeks began to seep from my body. Even my bones had been concealing stress. Surely one misstep would have snapped me in two. My pieces falling to the floor would have broken into a zillion fragments and scattered on the disinfected hospital linoleum.

After our respite, it was time for the dirty work. I had to change Matthew's diaper, weigh it, and jot down this earth-shaking information. The thirty minutes we had been locked together also had to be recorded. Though how does one measure a mother's milk, unless she has see-through breasts, with ounces marked in increments?

I handled Matthew much as I would a delicate china doll. He seemed so fragile and unbelievably pale. His porceline skin a neon sign to alert everyone who entered his cubicle that all was not quite right. Just being in ICU did that.

They're not called bouncing babies for nothing. I'm sure it's because they bounce back so quickly from everything, not just illness and surgery. When a child gets a fever it's like the end of their world. They lie around looking so pathetic that if they were horses, we would have to shoot them. Their big round eyes stare so pitifully that we would do anything to take away their pain. Then, within a short time, they surprise us by running up the walls and doing flips onto the sofa. Now that we are ready for a long, undisturbed rest ourselves.

Matthew was being moved to join the regular patients down on the seventh floor. No more of this one-patient-to-every-nurse business. This demotion was actually a sign that he was recovering well, even rapidly. Good-bye to intensive care and hello to overworked, overwrought nurses. I hope you have time for the two dozen new patients we are shipping you today.

An orderly came to fetch us and I stuffed all our belongings under Matthew's gurney and grabbed the foot of his bed. While the orderly pushed, I pulled, and we continued in this fashion to the elevator. With his expertise, we managed to wedge ourselves in the conveyor and took a short ride down three floors.

It was a different world. The hustle and bustle nearly bowled me over. My ears were attuned to the hushed atmosphere of intensive care. I wasn't accustomed to such a din. People pushed and rushed about hurrying to do something terribly important. I followed the orderly's lead to our assigned spot on the ward and we transferred Matthew to a regular crib. The gurney would be returned to surgery.

The requisite ten days post-op became five. They were five long days of army-like routine and change. Change his dressing, change his diaper and change the sheets. With all the change it seemed nothing would ever be the same. I had never reached so deeply or had a comparable level of suffering. My perception shifted, and with my new outlook, a revised world came into focus. Matthew was healing so quickly that they soon changed his release to Monday, coincidentally a federal election day in Canada. I was in a fever to have my son discharged.

We raced home just under the speed limit, stopping at the school to vote. While Mike waited in the car, I faced the driving rain and determinedly made my way into the building. Nothing could have prevented me from casting my ballot. I was still alive, we had survived and I had power. I voted Liberal yet again. I voted to have a normal life, and satisfied I took a short ride home.

4
LIFE AFTER SURGERY

The crisis was over and now it was time for us to come together as a family. It was our first night home. Mike had gone back to the office he had neglected while tending to his wife and child in the hospital. He brushed my cheek with his lips and gave me a one armed hug.

"You'll be fine. No more blinking machines, no more strangers running our lives."

I closed the door firmly behind him and went to lie on the couch. Matthew was having his afternoon nap and I burrowed deeper into the orange and rust checks of my living room sofa. What exactly was I supposed to do while he was sleeping? I couldn't possibly sleep myself and miss something. I lay there for two hours in a virtual coma, with bones so weary and muscles so achy from the stress of the past few weeks that when Matthew actually awoke, I was paralyzed for what seemed like an eternity. I eventually pulled myself up and lurched toward the nursery.

Matthew had both feet in the air near his face and was sucking his big toe. What an accomplishment. I wished I could do the same. He released his foot from his mouth and valiantly strained until he flipped over onto his stomach. He seemed quite proud. I picked him up and cradled him in my arms. I brought him back into the living room and opened my shirt – actually, it was Mike's shirt, as mine were too small. I offered him a breast and frantically hoped he would take it. Nursing had become quite a challenge and I was never sure if he would eat. He was just getting his third tooth, too early, and was finicky. His cheeks blazed like two hot cherry tomatoes as he proceeded to bite my nipple with three teeth, including the just erupted third front tooth. Immediate reactions are not always the most rational, but I tapped him on the nose like a naughty puppy chewing a good pair of shoes and told him firmly no, all the while biting back my own tears. I don't advise anyone to try this at home, but it worked for me.

He didn't sleep well that night. He would doze for a couple of hours and wake up. I wasn't giving him any night feedings. As he was over three months old, I was heeding the recommendations of the "experts," to give only a bottle of boiled water to settle him. My baby wouldn't allow me the indulgence of a full night's rest until he was over seven months old. And this was only after I took him to the pediatrician for his checkup, who ordered me to sleep away from the baby to get some peace. She must have noticed me stretched out in the waiting room across three metal chairs and my inability to rise when his name was called. She made me promise to let Mike take over for several nights to give me a chance to catch up.

My husband very generously agreed to watch our son alone while I slept in my father's apartment/office. I gratefully dragged myself upstairs, put on a nightgown, pulled down the blind, and then finally, blissfully fell asleep for ten beautiful hours. Unbeknownst to the sleeping beauty, prince charming had a much different time of it. Matthew cried for most of the night, and Mike told me he had to rock him in his carriage for over two hours while he lay in bed. He was exhausted. His appreciation for me had taken a quantum leap by morning. He gladly relinquished his temporary hold on the primary parent role.

Matthew's stitches were healing nicely except for the knot at the end. It was an angry red and seemed to be seeping. The doctor prescribed an antibiotic and a salve. I needed them to work. We were flying to Toronto for Christmas.

As the plane began to gather speed, I realized that just as my ears would certainly become blocked as we approached higher altitudes, so would a baby's. I quickly whipped out one of my milkers and roused an almost sleeping infant. He latched on, drained the breast, and averted possible painful popping in his ears. I couldn't have borne to have him suffer one more drop of pain.

Visiting family over the holidays can be joyous, in the movies or literary fiction. Reality can be a strain. We stayed with Helga and Gary, a couple we had met on our honeymoon four years earlier. I was waiting in the main lounge of the Guadeloupe Club Med on the Wednesday after our wedding. I remember it was a Wednesday because Gary pointed out a fabulous woman on the photo board that day, and the next day, and the next, and always called her "Wednesday." It became a standing joke in our relationship: "Remember Wednesday. Wasn't she beautiful?" I think he even purchased her picture.

I was sitting for a few minutes watching an even more attractive brunette sipping a drink a few tables over. She was wearing a red halter dress and had just few enough freckles to be charming. A gentleman purposefully walked towards me, and as he brushed by my table, I touched his arm and motioned towards the bella-donna.

"Isn't she beautiful?"

He beamed. "That's my wife," he said.

Gary and Helga are attractive, successful and childless, which doesn't preclude an understanding that babies are noisy, but I naively wanted to keep the baby quiet. We had been assigned the guest bedroom in their suburban cottage. They had just built the house and as yet had not furnished our sleeping quarters or the living room. The former had a double air mattress and a lamp on the floor, and the latter had three garden chairs and a ridiculously expensive stereo system. Matthew was arranged on the floor in his traveling crib and would let us know loudly and longly that he did not like traveling. After traveling with a baby, neither did I. Shushing and cooing did nothing. He refused all offers of breast and bottle. He was determined to ruin his parent's snoozing and succeeded, but fortunately our hosts were sound sleepers, or at least very polite.

I had my ritual: baby fed and fussed over, nerves put on alert for that dependable cry in the dark. This time it never came. I stayed on edge until the dull morning cracked its way through to my consciousness. The next evening was a repeat of the first, and I awoke a little more refreshed and twigging to the possibility that this could become a trend. Not so, since Matthew followed his performance with a night of horror. Perhaps I'm exaggerating … but no, it was excruciating: he cried and dozed and it was more of the same. But the next evening Matthew actually slept and he kept on doing it for the next twenty years. It was to me, and I'm sure to desperate parents everywhere, a minor miracle. Maybe not up there with ridding a sinner of leprosy, but sleep is very important to me and doing without makes me very grouchy. So much so, that as I recovered my equilibrium, I slowly acknowledged that perhaps my relationship with *what's his name* had slipped on my list of priorities. It was time to push him back on top. When was the last time he had been on top?

My weight hadn't completely returned to pre-baby numbers, but I was definitely more svelte than I had been four days after the C-section. Then, when I finally waddled my way to the scale, I learned I was one hundred and ninety-three pounds. I stood on the scale and cried. I feared I would never be slim again. For goodness sake, I had had the baby. What was the problem?

Walking and general baby care removed another thirty or so pounds. I was feeling pretty good and thought I looked sexy, although Mike never seemed to be interested and my efforts at seduction would always fall flat. In

the past I had tried new lingerie, sleek nighties and can-
dle-lit baths. I'd even greeted him at the door wrapped
in Saran wrap. Bedroom gymnastics were not part of our
nighttime routine. If it wasn't first thing in the morning,
my chances of getting lucky were pretty slim. Even con-
ceiving Matthew took some work.

About two months before I had gotten pregnant I
missed a birth control pill. Even though I desperately
wanted a baby, this was not premeditated: my sister had
moved my prescription and only told me where it was
the next morning. As I later discovered, I am extremely
fertile and that was all it took. Once I was expecting, I
was ecstatic. Then I crashed. I had a miscarriage six
weeks later. I took to crying steadily for the next forty-
eight hours, until Michael pleaded with me to stop. He
promised we'd have another baby.

So against medical advice to wait another couple of
months (my doctor didn't know my husband) I grabbed
Mike the minute he walked in the door on the first day
I could possibly be ovulating and threw him on the bed.
Don't mess with a hormonal woman. Six hours later,
after doing the bicycle with my legs up in the air and
propping my hips up on two pillows for hours to avoid
spillage, I heard a magical bell sound in my head. I knew
I was pregnant. Matthew was born August 9, 1985. I
had been right.

Sex still wasn't happening often enough, but I grew
somewhat accustomed to Mike's disinterest. Besides, I
had something new to occupy myself with. We bought a
house, a gorgeous model home that I knew I would buy
even as I walked in the door. I pulled out my checkbook

in the vestibule and put down a deposit in the first ten minutes. It was a split-level bungalow with a fireplace in the massive family room. The kitchen had forty-three oak cabinets and ceramic tile. It was so beautiful that I knew we would be very happy there. I was wrong.

Matthew took sick again and we rushed him once more to the Montreal Children's Hospital. We thought he had a hernia. His groin was distended and he was in distress. Our doctor in emergency was Dr. Laberge, our surgeon for Matthew's lobectomy. He reassured us that it wasn't a hernia but a hydroseal, which mimics the symptoms of a hernia. Fortunately, it didn't require another surgery. We had been spared.

Once at home I gave my son a cookie just to enjoy watching him eat. He held the teething biscuit tightly in his fist and sucked both ends until the goopy mess dissolved, then he worked his way into the heart of his palm. Later I put him down on the wood floor of the family room and turned on his fire truck. He echoed every squeal that fire truck made and then some. Matthew had a wide range of funny noises, shrieks and bellows that ended with his aaah noises as he went off to sleep. He wasn't quite crawling but he managed to follow his fire truck sporadically, though usually in a backwards slide. Matthew was off the height charts and quite a respectable 78% on the weight chart. He was growing fast.

Sleep was no longer the hot button topic that it had been previously, but it was still a priority, for him and for me. He took two naps a day, and though he was sleeping through the night with some *regularity* – what a wonderful word – I was silly enough to rock him off to dreamland every night in his infant carrier.

Matthew was upstairs in his crib watching me in the kitchen. It was a record-breaking day in terms of temperature, the warmest April 1 in a hundred and fifteen years. The sky was an unbroken dome of deep blue that was gloriously, perfectly springtime. I was cleaning: dusting, wiping, shaking out and scrubbing. Clearing the house and my mind of the cobwebs and clutter that had settled in for a long winter's rest.

With cleanliness and order came clarity. One can only clean for so long before the truth of the situation becomes clear. Michael and I were losing what little intimacy we had. Our relationship, besides being not very physical, was not one of shared confidences either. We both liked to travel, go to movies and out to dinner, but a deeper connection was never quite pulled off.

After living in the new house for about a year with a healthy toddler of eighteen months, I was noticing some subtle changes in my husband, when I wasn't too busy running after Matthew. If I asked Matthew, "Is that your Daddy?" or "Where's your Daddy?" he would look all around and head for the stairs. Though when the real thing actually came home, it was another matter. Often when Mike was getting in, Matthew would come crawling and shrieking towards him, only to reach for something on the floor next to him.

Matthew learned to throw a ball, a talent he used to great advantage with a basketball, shattering a blown glass figurine of a clown that my mother had dragged home from California. Although Matthew was now well, we did have another episode of illness that entailed a hospital visit, a fever of 105° F, two ear infections, penicillin, twelve or thirteen spots (depending on who's doing the counting) and finally, a diagnosis of roseola. He was very irritable throughout the entire episode.

Matthew was a delight in so many ways. He hid behind curtains, in cupboards and the hall closet, until we would say, "Where's Matthew?" He pulled out all the shoes from the closet and didn't put any back. He chewed gum and I taught him how to stick out his tongue. He talked a lot and told me to "go away" to make me cry. He was a beautiful, happy child that lit up my life and every day I was grateful for him. Every night, when I tucked him in, I would say, "Thank you for being my boy."

As a very active toddler Matthew managed some interesting flips down stairs and falls off curbs. He seemed to always be scraping, banging and bleeding. Especially around his mouth, where there were too many blood vessels that were particularly susceptible in a fall. And learning to walk meant he fell a lot. Nothing would ever be as serious as his hospitalizations and surgery. I learned to take it easy and not get wound up. He would make it and so would I.

I knew something was happening in our marriage when I noticed my husband was sleeping on a cot at the office some nights and coming home late on others. This was after a trip he took alone to England, and I had terrible dreams the entire week of us never being together. His behavior shift had either been slow in coming or I had been slow in recognizing the signs. He started buying himself clothes, after years of me bringing things home from the department store. He changed the way he styled his hair and began going out in the evening with his younger brother and his girlfriend. I was specifically uninvited, even though I had fixed those two up in the first place.

One evening stands out painfully from the many other nights. I had embarrassed myself once more by imploring Mike to take me with him to the bar. He stood in front of the mirror, combing his (thinning) hair with his fingers, and without even looking at me said, "No." He was not interested in what I had to say and didn't seem fazed by my hurt feelings.

Time has the elastic capacity to pass at a speed indirectly related to how quickly you want it to. That evening I wanted him to be home before he even stepped out on me. I sat my (not as big as it used to be) bottom on the love seat in the living room and waited. Matthew was asleep after expending the energy of a small nuclear power plant, as he did every day. I sat waiting for Mike's return. As each car turned the corner towards our end of the street, my muscles tightened and my jaw clenched. As each car passed my house, my tension released another cascade of tears. My nose had been clogged for more than two hours and my eyes were puffy. After one in the morning, I realized that perhaps he would not even come home.

He returned shortly before 2 a.m. and was surprised to see me galloping down the stairs to the entrance by the garage. He held up a hand and gave me a stern look.

He was dead sober. It seemed there was nothing to talk about.

Looking back, I suppose that there was never anything we had talked about. We dated for over five years before he finally married me, and even then we never really knew each other at all. I had used threats, tears and manipulation techniques to get that man down the aisle – it had never been his idea. It took many hard lessons for me to learn that life goes more smoothly when you don't force it, when you accept with grace the challenges that come your way. You just can't put the toothpaste back in the tube.

The rest of the summer continued with sporadic periods of relative calm. We traveled most weekends to Mike's parent's country place in Vermont and planned an extended stay for the end of July. I was even to have a mother's-helper for the entire week and hired a seventeen-year-old named Paul. I had great expectations for this vacation. Quiet walks with just the two of us while Nanny watched Matthew, a round of golf, dinner out, perhaps with champagne, and maybe, just possibly, some sex. Good, old-fashioned, rollicking married sex. Is that an oxymoron?

We had spent the night of our wedding at the "cottage" in Vermont. We pulled in around 1 a.m., exhausted and excited, and stumbled and giggled our way to the Jacuzzi room. Well, I stumbled and giggled, Mike was fine. We found a congratulatory note along with a chilled bottle of our favourite champagne. After a sexy bubble bath, it was time for bed in the yellow room, the room usually reserved for guests. I donned my white peignoir set and watched my new husband rapidly fall asleep and start to snore rhythmically with a slow and gentle rumble. It was then that I had my first premonition that all was not quite so perfect as I had thought. As I stared bleakly at the man with whom I had just signed all those legal documents, and whom I had sworn to love and all that jazz in front of all those witnesses, I wondered, "Who is he and what have I gotten myself into?"

Make that a second premonition. From the minute we had gotten engaged, which was at my insistence, I had my doubts. I negotiated for months with myself about how we would still be able to return the ring and get the money back if I broke it off. How in the weeks leading up to the wedding day I had ground my teeth so much at night that I worried about having only stubs left in my mouth to marry him with. The night before the wedding my future grandmother-in-law slipped me a little blue sleeping pill, and even that could not steady my nerves, still my teeth or allow me to sleep. The next day, as my father drove me to the church on time, only one thought rattled around in my head: "You can still get out of it." There I was, putting on my lipstick in my dad's old Monte Carlo, driving down Beaconsfield Boulevard, and all I could think about was how I could get out of it. It was my idea. I literally cried, pleaded and begged for years, told the poor guy to make up his mind or get lost. What exactly had been my problem?

We had been going up to the cottage since before we married, though we went less often when the baby arrived. Mid-week of our vacation found me lounging by the pool while my mother's-helper watched Matthew.

Actually we both watched and didn't watch at the same time. We each thought the other was more alert than was the case. Matthew chose that moment to jump into the pool, wearing a flotation device around his waist. He jumped from one corner of the stairs to the other and landed on his teeth. With his mouth wide open yelling for joy, he had managed to knock out all six upper front teeth. Or so we thought, as we frantically and alternately looked for missing teeth and attempted to staunch the blood. Now Matthew was really screaming and I think I may have been too. Mike was quite calm in a crisis and as he held our son, I called my dentist back in Canada. He told us to relax and to bring in Matthew for a check.

I drove home with Paul, leaving the unfortunate, tormented lad pale and sorrowful on his doorstep. I then learned that rather than scattering upon impact, the teeth had been pushed back into the gums and could be expected to return in about six weeks, which they promptly did.

Three days later, Mike was quieter than usual on the drive back from Vermont. As I questioned and badgered him in ever-increasing desperation, I came to understand that we were over. He was unhappy, I was confused and when we got home I asked him to leave. Thus began our separation.

5
THE DIVORCE

Being separated was something I had never really experienced. Mike and I had broken up once before for a short while and I had been the one to do the deed then. I found a new boyfriend while he was out West skiing. This was something new and utterly beyond my ken. Mike asked me, "Could we try being apart but not see other people?"

The entire process of getting unmarried was surreal. Mike would show up to visit Matthew wearing a new shirt or pair of pants and I would feel another tear in the fabric of our life. That sense of belonging to one another was fast disappearing and in its place was suspicion. Was he seeing someone else? I had always been sensitive to the feeling of being replaced in my husband's affections. He steadfastly denied that there was anyone else and continued to do so even just a few years ago, long past when it still mattered. One particular night he was over for a visit and upstairs in Matthew's bedroom playing on the floor. His jacket was slung over a kitchen chair with the lapel thrown back and the inside pocket peeking out. I was unable to stop my evil twin from going through his pockets and taking a cursory look in his wallet. I found a phone number in his left pocket. I don't remember the name on the slip but I do remember how terribly guilty I felt while doing the snooping.

Michael moved out on July 27, just before Matthew's second birthday. Could our son's infection and near death, his lung surgery and other health problems have contributed to our drifting apart? I have to believe that everything, without exception, happens for a reason and by some grand design. There are no coincidences in life. There are choices and serendipity.

I was still not working, but I needed to do something. I took a job on Saturday nights to avoid those long weekends of being alone, now that I was an unwilling single mother. I waitressed at a four star restaurant that catered to weddings in its newly built addition. That was just the ticket for a recently separated woman. My girl-friend Kathy asked me to be her matron of honour at the same time and couldn't understand why I wasn't happier for her. I honestly tried my best but it had been only two weeks since my husband had left me.

At first, I was living in denial and not accepting the situation. One morning in early December I awoke and looked outside, finally perceiving that winter had arrived. In my mind, as part of my unreal separation, it was still July 27, the day my husband had left. Time seemed to stand still.

Michael always played touch football and I had been his number one fan. Every year from August to November, I was usually the only wife present at every game. In the rain, in the burning sun and sometimes in the early snow, I yelled and cheered so long and loud that I became the team mascot. So this year I was a little lost when there was no one to cheer for and unaware of the passage of time. Autumn had always meant going to Mike's games, so when I didn't, it remained July. Winter didn't come until that cold, bleak morning when I acknowledged the snow and with it the arrival of my new status. I was no one's fan now.

I admit to being naïve. If someone tells me something, I'll believe it. Mike said, "It will only be a trial separation, I hope we'll get back together," and I believed him. He came over almost every day and looked after Matthew at our house every Saturday night, while I slept at my father's apartment after working at the restaurant. He always seemed happy to see me and would kiss me hello and good-bye. He took me out for my twenty-ninth birthday the week before Christmas and bought me a set of intricately detailed jewel boxes. We had the occasional date and I hoped he would come home soon.

New Year's Eve found me working and getting a sweet midnight kiss from hunky Jean-Pierre, a fellow waiter. I wished it had been Mike. The days passed with interminable slowness and yet suddenly it was Valentine's day, a day for lovers. And a fabulous day to reconcile, one would surmise. It was Sunday morning and I awoke late after working, serving lovers until 2 a.m. the previous night. I was in the mood to serve my own lover that day and called home to talk to my husband. He was apparently in a good mood.

"When do you think we might get back together?" I asked him. It had been over six months, long enough for him to make up his mind.

Mike hesitated before answering. "I've made up my mind," he said, "and I won't be coming back."

The cliché "my heart sank" doesn't do justice to the way my heart took a hundred storey nose-dive down an elevator shaft with a snapped cable upon hearing the news. I hurried back to our house to confront the man who had promised to love, honour and obey me just seven years earlier. He was standing in the bedroom with a suitcase filled with the remainder of his things. Never one to talk about anything important, he just shook his head and brushed past me on his way out to the car. I didn't hear from him for the next two days and had no way to contact him. He later told me he drove to Ottawa in a daze and spent the night before returning to Montreal.

Things began to move swiftly after the question of reconciliation was settled. He called me to say that we could stay married and travel together, but not live together. Although not mentioned, I understood the implication was that we were free to see other people. I don't think he ever had an inkling of what I was about. That scenario was utterly impossible for me to digest, and I told him so.

"I could never consider such a sham of a marriage and I'll be getting a divorce as quickly as possible."

Now he was shocked.

"What's your hurry?" he asked.

"I'm only twenty-nine. I want to remarry and have more children."

Mike eventually conceded the validity of my situation and we came to terms easily. We used the same lawyer, told him we had been separated for over a year, and soon had a date for a divorce that fall. We arrived at a fair agreement, even though I was more interested in being nice than protecting my rights. I wanted to get along so that Matthew wouldn't have to see his parents fight. I could have fought and possibly gotten more than I did, but I didn't.

I sold the house within two weeks, making a tidy profit that we split evenly. I moved into a much smaller townhouse on a neat crescent. Choosing a home in February is never a good idea, as the snow in Canada can hide a number of flaws – in my case, the absence of a paved driveway.

The move itself was the most difficult part of the divorce. The day started out okay, with Mike and his brother helping me to pack and bring everything to the new house. As the day wore on I gradually began to understand that this was really the end. The end of all my dreams of a happy marriage and of the future I had envisioned of us together until we were old and grey. It all came crashing down with a thump. I collapsed upstairs in the new house in the corner of my new empty bedroom. I was crying and sweating in an uncontrollable heap and Michael didn't know what to do with me. He called his mother and she came to my rescue. She talked to me calmly and helped me into her car. She then drove me to my friend Kathy's house and left me there to sob in peace. Mike finished the move without me, almost certainly relieved that I wasn't there.

Within a couple of days I realized that I would have to open some boxes if I were to have some sort of a life. So I took myself into the room with the most boxes and turned on the radio. Standing in my new kitchen with maple veneer cabinets and barely enough space for a table, I faced my new reality. I was about ready to have a full wallow in the poor-MEs, when a very lively tune came on the radio – "Footloose," from the movie starring Kevin Bacon. I was invigorated, hopeful, joyful and footloose. I began to dance around my kitchen. Those boxes were emptied and put away before that feeling went away.

Part of me desperately wanted Mike back. Feelings of love and commitment don't disappear when one half of the couple wants out. I still loved him and would have done anything, up to and including ironing his shirts, to win him back. But he would have none of it. He didn't want me touching his laundry or anything else.

One early evening the following summer, after I had just finished a softball game, I saw Mike drive past in a Porsche with another woman. I had never, ever, felt so weird before. Part of me was incensed to see my husband tooling about town with another woman in tow. And where did he get a Porsche?

The sensible part of me accepted the reality of our separation and that he was free to do what he wanted. The part of me that didn't think at all, and that did most of the talking, began to follow – not too closely, of course. They drove down the boulevard towards the lake. As they turned onto a side street, I kept up for another hundred yards, until I stopped and went home. What exactly would I have done when they arrived at their destination? A confrontation would have been pointless and made me look even smaller than I already felt. He had moved on and I had stayed behind.

Matthew was aware that something had changed. I found him hitting his father's picture and saying, "Bad daddy." I asked him if he was mad. He was. I explained that Daddy loved him very much no matter where he lived. I told Matthew that I knew he missed his father, but that hopefully we would both get used to not having him around.

It was wonderful being Matthew's mother. He was very sweet, but there were so many times when I could have given him to his father, because I just couldn't take it anymore. Then I would look at his face and his earnest way about him, and I was the happiest mother on the crescent.

Matthew woke up every hour the entire night for weeks and often skipped a nap after the separation. Mike and I both tried to be supportive and loving. He continued to visit almost every day and took Matthew on some weekends.

With the date of the divorce getting closer, I felt stronger and more certain. Of course, there were periods when it all seemed bizarre. Like when Mike's younger sister got married and I wasn't invited. We were still married and I was sitting at home feeding Matthew a chicken and broccoli dinner that he didn't want to eat and I hadn't wanted to cook. Every morsel I forced on him made me cry. It felt so unfair. Why wasn't I there? Who had taken my place? I was really on the outside looking in now. I was no longer family.

After supper, I sat at the top of the stairs and began to sob. Matthew, always a tender, sympathetic sort, came and sat on my lap. He held my face in his hands and asked me not to cry, because it was making him sad. I did stop for his sake and tried, somewhat successfully, not to break down in front of him anymore. It scared him and caused him uncertainty. It made me feel hopeless and without direction. I actually got quite low at one point and thought about ending my life. I even came up with a method. I was going to barricade myself in the garden shed with a running lawn-mower and asphyxiate myself. The plan wasn't feasible since the walls of the shed had cracks and holes large enough to ram a lawn mower through. Besides, I could never leave my son. I called my girlfriend Myrna, who wouldn't let me do it and who would have been extremely mad at me if I did. I don't think I was ever serious to the point of actually committing suicide, but it was a running theme for a few months that were both dark and enlightening.

My marriage ended not with an explosion but with a fizzle that perfectly defined our lackluster life together. We had mixed with all the combustion of mud and baking soda. We had been as exciting as fireworks under water. We had ended not with a bang but with a feeble whimper.

Mike found himself an apartment in an exclusive building that seemed to be full of divorced daddies. I took all the furniture, dishes and wedding presents, including those from his side of the family. I made him an album with pictures from the twelve years we were together, though most of them were of Matthew. I also circled on a calendar his friends and family members' birthdays so that he could keep track – that had always been my responsibility. There were times when it seemed that maybe Mike was having second thoughts, but for me it was fait accompli. All we had to do was sign the papers.

October 4, 1988, was a grey day devoid of lightness, the pavement slick with rain. Mike arrived to drive me to court in Old Montreal for the visit before the judge. He pulled up in his new sports car, another gift to himself, and opened the door for me. Michael was always the gentleman and quite polite too. He had never hit me or even raised his voice, but he could get angry. It was a rare, freak occurrence, but when he blew, watch out. His temper was like a visiting comet – something to see. Only once did he rough me up slightly by grabbing me by the shirtfront and lifting me off the floor. He stopped and walked away, eyes bulging. I was never afraid of being hurt physically but I was neglected emotionally and I could have used a bit more affection. Hell, I could have used a lot more.

We drove in silence. We waited outside the court-room until our names were called. We stood before the judge and listened to him state that he was granting us a divorce. This was after he confirmed my sole custody of Matthew, Michael's visitation rights and monthly pay-ments, and other arrangements agreed upon with our lawyer. What a bargain he had been at only eight hundred dollars. I was wearing a beige silk dress with large cream polka dots. I found my divorce dress at a battered women's shelter that I visited while I waited for my brother Anthony to finish shingling the roof. I stuffed a large paper bag full of really great clothes for only one dollar. That was even more of a bargain than my pathetic lawyer.

The return trip was unremarkable, but Mike's behavior when we arrived at my townhouse was certainly unexpected. He parked in my driveway and walked me to the door. I asked him in for a cup of coffee. After I prepared the coffee, I went upstairs to change out of my dress and heels. He followed me to my bedroom. I was emotionally drained from our ordeal in court and told him to stay downstairs. He continued to march on up. I went in my room, closed the door and locked it.

"We're divorced now," I reminded him. "You'd better leave."

Perhaps he wanted what he could no longer have. Maybe he wanted closure. I showed him closure by remaining barricaded in my room until he left. He stormed out, the tension of the day having its effect on him too.

I stayed on my bed for several hours. The impending dusk caused a riot of autumnal colour to fill the room. The season was well suited to my pensive mood. The leaves were dying, dead and rotting. I felt on the inside what I saw on the outside. All my dreams for my marriage and my future had been trampled on. I was disillusioned and now, it seemed, very much divorced.

6

LIFE AFTER SEX

I couldn't really miss what I wasn't having. I adjusted tentatively to my new single status. I returned to work after my ex-husband – that moniker was much easier than calling him *husband* had been on our honeymoon – declared his intentions on Valentine's day. I went back to my father's insurance business working part-time, with Tuesdays off. He was ecstatic to have me back and was very comforting.

I returned to an old love by taking skiing lessons with a ski school every Tuesday. They would drive a busload of us up to various hills throughout the season, from December to March. My father wanted so much to make me feel better that he paid my fees and bought all my new equipment. I think the divorce made him very sad, though I don't think he missed Michael all that much. During our marriage he had sensed that something was never quite right.

When I came home from shopping one day, after not buying anything and still positively glowing about some sheets I had seen, my father gave me money to return and buy the set and the matching comforter. Funny thing about those sheets. When I finally saw Michael's new apartment and took a peek at the bedroom, I was stunned to see that he had copied my brass bed, complete with the same sheets. When I casually mentioned the coincidence, Michael said that he hadn't noticed.

"But I showed them to you just last week and even mentioned where I had got them," I ventured further.

Michael soon changed the subject and I never brought it up again, but I wondered for a very long time about the Freudian significance of his replication.

Just before the divorce I met a priest. He was a counselor at a women's shelter and we fell to talking. I told him I was getting a divorce and felt lost. Whereupon he gave me some wonderful advice: "Give yourself some time to be alone before jumping into another relationship, or even casual dating. Try about eighteen months."

I told him that sounded like forever.

While I managed to avoid getting serious with anyone for the next year-and-a-half, I found ways to date a few times during my supposed isolation. This was after many, many nights of talking to the empty spot in the bed next to me and asking it, "Where's the guy that's supposed to be here?"

My search began soon thereafter, three months post-divorce and after enduring about a year alone.

One of the first fellows I went out with was named Steve. When we were in high school together, he was considered one of the "cool" guys and was very good looking, though a little on the height-challenged side. I ran into him at a local bar and he asked me out for the following Thursday. I accepted an invitation to dinner. Thursday was *the* night to party in Montreal, and though I wasn't much into the club scene, I was thrilled to be going to downtown Montreal to a place aptly named: "Thursdays." I arranged overnight babysitting for Matthew with my sister Lorraine and had an hour to prepare before Steve would be at my door. I fretted over my clothes, all of which seemed outdated and I was sure were just plain ugly. I finally settled on an outfit that camouflaged my zaftig hips and accentuated my god-given attributes. Namely, a black skirt that allowed my really good legs to show and a top that gave him some cleavage to ponder.

Steve arrived promptly and we were soon at the restaurant seated by a window. I had a great view of the activity below on the street and looked around the room enjoying the attractive sights. Steve was worth looking at and we had a pleasant evening. I ordered steak tartar for the first and last time, and after trying raw hamburger meat, I was ready to try anything. Steve was not. He didn't try anything after dinner. He never even called back. It looked like this dating thing was going to be hard work.

Another fellow I met was an engineer named Sylvain. We connected on a ski hill north of Montreal. I spied him in the great room of the lodge and was entranced by his muscular body and shiny, shaved head. He loved to laugh and asked me for my telephone number. Imagine that, a guy asked me for my number. I floated all the way home, and can you believe it, he even called. He took me out for a couple of lovely dinners and then to a company party at a racquet club. I was the only English-speaking person in a room of one hundred and fifty. When they were all piled on the dance floor they took to singing and mangling every song the DJ played, in English of course. That was funny enough, but the icing on the muffin came when he played the Chicken Dance. Does this song get played anywhere else in the world besides French Canadian wedding receptions and parties? You have not lived until you have witnessed forty or fifty sober and not so sober adults flapping and clucking around like chickens to a polka-like beat.

When he took me home it was obvious he wanted to have sex. Even though I had always held out before, sometimes up to three months, I was so confused and lacking in any kind of sexual validation that I took him upstairs and let him have a go. We tried it in the shower but it just wasn't working for me. He tried in my bed but I was too distracted by his absolute lack of rhythm. It reminded me of the chicken dance. We were both relieved when he left and I was glad when he never called back. Our lack of cohesiveness and sexual satisfaction was very disturbing. I was worried it could become a trend.

There was a man who called me after hearing I was newly single. His name was David. When I was eleven I had become friends with his sister. He had been eight at the time. Our age difference had lessened over time and he charmed me over the phone. I was even considering going out with him when his conversation rambled into the bizarre and he started bad mouthing his own recently discarded spouse. He had begun to divulge personal details of which I had no business and utterly no interest in knowing, when I cut him off and ended it before it even started.

Roger was the most successful of my casual dates and was a friend at a time when I needed one. He was of medium height with a body builder's physique, including a strong jaw and the cutest ears. His were the first ears I ever licked and it drove him crazy. We never ended up being physically intimate, but he served as a bridge for me, a transition from being married to being unmarried. We played squash, ate out and stayed in watching television. He met Matthew and seemed comfortable around my son. Matthew would always go up to his room when Roger came over. The third and last time he was there, Matthew said, "I want my Daddy, no Roger." That was enough for me. I had gained confidence and was prepared to move forward alone.

I couldn't screw up enough courage to place a personal ad in the newspaper but I did answer a few. One fellow was short, squat and had wispy hair. He lied about everything from his age to his appearance. Another was an Egyptian with teeth that protruded and looked like crooked Chiclets gum. He really wanted to be my friend. The third guy of the sad bunch was self-involved and managed to have a conversation throughout our date without me. He never asked me anything about myself and only responded if he was the topic.

My mother had become quite worried by this point and got involved. She took some photographs of me near the lake to be submitted to a dating agency. Unfortunately I had just had a permanent done to my naturally wavy hair and was looking a little frazzled. It had been a wonderfully sunny day and I squinted and pouted as sexily as I could into my mother's camera lens. My mother also paid my hefty registration fee as a means to ensure my compliance with her wishes. She wanted me married or at least dating, since it tore her up to see me so unhappy.

The dating agency was downtown and I went to the interview with apprehension and some misgivings. The woman assigned to my file seemed confident and capable. Surely she would find someone for me. She badgered me with utterly useless questions for forty minutes and flipped through files for twenty more. She produced three names with accompanying pictures and I chose the most handsome one. His name was Simon.

Simon had a British accent that would have charmed the boots off Puss in Boots and managed to continue in a most engaging manner throughout the evening. He charmed me back to his place, even though his bragging about his BMW (it was old and it was orange!) was definitely off-putting. We settled in the living room of his tiny row house and he gave me a liqueur to sip. He asked me if I shaved my genital area. I choked on my liqueur.

"What?"

He repeated his question. "Do you shave down there?"

Now I'd been married, I'd been divorced and I had even given birth for what that's worth, but I could still be considered a naïve, even gullible woman. When Simon hit me with such a vulgar, personal question on a first date, I got up and left. I almost staggered to my car where I pondered two things. Why would he ask me such a thing, and why would anyone ever do such a thing to themselves?

Simon never called back. Maybe if I had answered him….

The realization that I was not dating club or personal ad material began to disturb my consciousness. I decided to call an old boyfriend, Brian. I knew him from high school, that endless supply of male energy, and we had dated briefly during a short sojourn when I had dumped Mike for a few weeks at age twenty. It was now almost ten years later and I suddenly couldn't put him out of my thoughts. I knew where he worked because I had seen him in a company truck. I managed to dial the number after looking it up in the telephone book, even though I was trembling and short of breath. He happened to be in and within minutes he was knocking on my door.

He looked better that I remembered: taller, blonder and more self-assured. He had filled out with a broader chest, though his hips were slim, giving him a V-shaped torso. He looked happier to see me than I could even have hoped for and we were emotionally connected in seconds, as if no time had lapsed between us. We went out for coffee and sat huddled for three hours. He never returned to work even though he worked, as I found out, for his live-in girlfriend's father. He confided to me that he was very dissatisfied with his present circumstance.

"We never have sex," he said. "She doesn't share my interests and is never affectionate with me."

I told him I'd had the same problem, but he didn't seem much interested in me except as a sounding board. Although most of me was enchanted, I also wondered why he would stay if he were as miserable as he clearly stated he was.

I invited Brian over that evening and introduced him to Matthew. I had studiously avoided many such meetings before this, but my chemicals ruled and lust prevailed. He was just so heavenly that I was already planning the wedding. He was stiff with my son and seemed to have the touch of a commandant. Brian even told me, after I had put my son to bed and read him a story, that I was too lenient with Matthew and that he seemed a bit spoiled. I chose to ignore his comments because he shortly thereafter removed his jeans on the pretext of showing me a scar on his chiseled thigh. It was at this point, after a bit of necking – it was lovely too – that I told him I couldn't in good conscience sleep with him while he was cohabiting with the loveless Carol. He should have tried begging or pleading but instead he donned his pants and left. I was left wondering.

The following evening he took the gallant step of telephoning my father and announcing that he would be dating his daughter. He called me after to say that he had asked his girlfriend to move out. I was ecstatic. I packed my bags for a previously planned weekend in Vermont with high spirits and every hope for a perfect future. I would see that man on Sunday.

I drove to Vermont to visit Floyd and his first annual jazz festival. It was being held on his large property and I was entitled to sleep in the big house, while most of the other guests were tenting it. Floyd was a world-renowned avian wood-carver and a good friend. He was also tall, blond and should have been my type but wasn't. I couldn't explain the lack of any fission on my part. Over the course of the weekend he certainly tried, but it was his Hungarian friend, Fek, from Connecticut, who absorbed my interest.

The festival was to be video-taped to make a documentary. Floyd was planning a bonfire for Saturday night that was already stacked twenty feet high in a teepee shape. There were a dozen groups scheduled to play and people crowded onto his sprawling acreage all day Friday. There was a twenty dollar admission fee, and black T-shirts with gold lettering announcing the event. I had one with "Staff" written on the back for those of us with privileged status – i.e. the use of indoor toilets and not the portable potties.

I drank too much beer on Saturday and after misjudging the ground while running barefoot, for what purpose I know not, I bent every toe under my feet into an awkward position that should have broken them but luckily didn't. I felt no pain that night, but the next morning it took several minutes to ascertain that it was my feet that hurt so terribly and that they were indeed purple. I hobbled around for another couple of hours and left for Montreal before lunch.

On the return trip I recalled some of the less pleasant details from my drunken foray the previous night. I dimly remembered flinging myself at an unwilling Hungarian whose only interest had been a beautiful European lass he barely knew who was returning home on Monday and to whom I'm sure he proposed that very night. I wasn't the only one drinking. A flash of Floyd, who followed me into the shower and said, "Can I wash your back?" caused me to shudder. I had rudely told him my back wasn't dirty and brushed him off. He was certainly being a poor host. I chuckled to myself and left all my misdeeds in Vermont.

It was such an uncharacteristic weekend that I chalked it up as a learning experience and willed myself home. Tucked in my bag was a blue T-shirt with a black and white cow and the word *Vermont* on it. It was practically the same electric blue as Brian's eyes and I couldn't wait to give it to him.

I waited for Brian at my dad's apartment, because I wasn't ready to go home to Matthew and Mike, who was babysitting at my place. Brian entered the office slowly through the already opened door. I had seen him pull up in the company truck and I was eagerly anticipating our reunion. He stood in front of me and told me that Carol had refused to move out. He had made his choice, he said. He wasn't going to force her to leave.

The coward would rather suffer than be forceful! He turned and walked down the stairs to his van. I was still holding his present. I couldn't absorb what he had said. It would appear that our affair was over before it had even begun. I was already regretting that I hadn't had sex with him when he had shown me his scar. Why had I been so high-minded, so honest? I should have given him what he wasn't getting at home. Our previous forays into the sexual arena had been highly charged, and though few and long ago, I remember that they were superlative. I sat in the office until the sun set and I was due home to relieve Mike.

I thanked him and pushed him out the door. Mike sputtered and hesitated, discombobulated by my unusual manner. Normally I was friendly and exchanged cheek kisses with him. I sent him packing with not so much as a good-bye. My behavior seemed to intrigue him, because he called me later and was all chummy. I didn't want to talk. I wanted to mourn my loss. I politely told him good-bye and returned to brooding in the dark.

It was time to change my attitude. Maybe I needed some professional help. I noted the telephone number and name of a psychiatrist on the bulletin board at the clinic where my son saw his pediatrician. I booked an appointment and showed up eagerly the following week. I was sure they would cure me or at least fix whatever was wrong. The nice lady doctor, after a few preliminary questions about myself and why I was there, told me quite frankly that I was fine but she sure would like to meet my husband. She recommended seeing a therapist to deal with my feelings and to help cope with the sadness that I felt. According to her, that was to be expected after the stress I had experienced.

Kathy was a registered nurse and a qualified family therapist; she was also my pediatrician's wife. When I entered her little office I immediately felt comforted. She was of medium stature with a flipped do of brown hair. She seemed serene, trustworthy and strong. Over the course of three sessions I told her all about my dead marriage, about coping with Matthew's illness and subsequent surgery and how inadequate and worthless I felt. I believed that no one would ever be interested in me because there was nothing interesting about me. My years with Mike and his detached manner had robbed me of self-esteem and I had allowed him to dictate how I felt about myself. I still spoke about him as if he was perfect and guiltless. It appeared that Mike had no fault with regard to the collapse of our relationship and I had shouldered full responsibility.

Kathy gently persuaded me that perhaps I had been looking at life with "rose-coloured glasses" and all the evidence suggested that she was right. This was definitely a breakthrough of sorts. By the third and last visit I had come to the healthy realization that I could be happy alone, without a man. That was surely something I had never considered before, as all my thoughts, actions, deeds and misdeeds had been predicated on having a man to complete me. How could I be happy or anything but miserable without a guy? She actually had me believing I could be happy alone. I went home with a smile on my face for the first time in a very long while. I was determined to be happy, damn happy, by myself.

7
Mom, I Met a Guy

This lasted all of two weeks, when I met HIM. It would seem that once you send a concrete thought out into the universe, such as the one I had recently projected about being thrilled about being alone, the great consciousness believes you and figures you've graduated to the next level. The universe decided I was finally ready to be happy *with* a man.

It could be that acceptance allows the problem to become a non-starter. Accepting my powerlessness over just about everything has allowed me an incredible freedom to just be. This was accomplished by having complete faith that I would be okay. The struggle to manipulate situations to my supposed desires would continue for a few more years. Eventually I would relinquish the power that I never had to begin with, even though it would take many more hard lessons to get it right. Flowing with the current of life has proved far easier than attempting to fight my way upstream.

I met Wayne the previous year on December 30 at the apartment of my sister Lorraine and her fiancé Paul. They were having an early New Year's Eve party and had invited some boys from St. Rose where Paul, for the most part, had grown up. I was still raw from my divorce proceedings two months before and I had just turned thirty on December 15.

That evening was also supposed to be the night I would meet my future husband according to a psychic I had visited in the days following my divorce. She had predicted I would meet someone on December 3 or 30, she wasn't sure which, and that he would be younger than I, have brown curly hair, blue eyes, glasses and would somehow be connected to Toronto. This information had left my brain after my December 3 visit to Toronto had failed to uncover anyone even remotely marriage material. It was only a year later that I found and read the transcripts from the psychic and realized that she had been bang on with the prediction.

I had made guacamole and was sitting in the living room when Wayne strutted in, accompanied by his two amigos, D'Arcy and Kerry. My sister introduced them to me and steered me towards D'Arcy in the misguided hope that we would like each other, hopefully a lot. Lorraine really cared for me and wanted me to find love. She had been disillusioned by the dissolution of my union with Mike.

The first thing I noticed was how young they were (Wayne would be twenty-four the following day) and how short all men seemed after having a tall husband. Wayne was actually a comfortable, no need to stretch five-foot-ten. Even though I hardly noticed him, he seemed to notice me. Every time I turned around that night there he would be. At my elbow or knee if I sat, always there. I only became aware of him after seeing him taste my guacamole and profusely compliment it. It was flattering to be mooned over by beautiful blue calf eyes. All the better to see them when he wasn't wearing his glasses, because he had broken a lens and had yet to replace it.

Six months later, on my baby sister's wedding day, I felt very good about myself and extremely happy for my sister. I had streaked my hair and was wearing a pink lacey dress that hugged my curves in a most satisfactory manner. I was to be her matron of honour. As I stood on the steps of the church after the ceremony, a familiar looking man came up to me and before he could re-introduce himself, I said, "You're Wayne, right?" He smiled a toothy grin, gratified that I had remembered him.

At the reception I was interested in a blond fellow named Todd, coincidentally Wayne's roommate. I danced a couple of dances with him and was hoping for a third when Wayne asked me to dance. We danced slow and close. We danced fast. We moved in perfect union. It was as if he could read my body and was able to adjust continually, to move in sync. Most amazing of all, he didn't even realize it. That we were in tune with each other was obvious even to observers. My aunt pulled me over after a particularly sweaty time of it and said, "You're going to marry that fellow."

To which I replied, "You're nuts."

I still preferred the blond Todd to the curly haired brunette. Wayne managed to ingratiate himself in a conversation with my mother and tried to pass himself off as a thirty-year-old lawyer. What a hoot! He certainly has plenty of the Irish blarney but he's no lawyer.

I have a photo of that evening that I treasure and that hangs in our bedroom. At the time, we were unaware that we were being photographed. Wayne was looking at me with a bemused smirk on his mug like he had my number and was going to take me home. I, meanwhile, look like I already knew what he was about and was ready to give him what for. It was a charming, wonderful moment that we were lucky enough to have documented, and people often remark that we appear to have known each other for years.

Wayne managed to drink a wee bit too much of the free scotch and I offered him a lift to my sister and new brother-in-law's apartment where the party promised to continue well into the night. My sister had decided to stay up until their flight the next morning at eight and was determined to have a bloody good time. I deposited Wayne on a chair in her living room, whereupon he began to snooze. I left immediately after that, because my idea of a good time is a good night's sleep. It wouldn't be long before that man gave me a follow-up call.

He got my number from my sister after they returned from their honeymoon. He called me on a day when I had had no plans for a long while and none in the foreseeable future. A free meal was hard to turn down.

He arrived on his motorcycle because he didn't own a car. We drove in my Chrysler hatchback to a restaurant by the water in Lachine where I had eaten on yet another failed date about a month before. I ordered the same meal, shrimp sautéed in Pernod, and listened as Wayne completely engaged me with his charm, wit and intelligence. He seemed slightly less intelligent when searching for the bathroom as he suavely careened into the kitchen only to be shooed out by the chef. I chuckled while he found the real washroom and attempted not to have noticed his miscue when he returned to the table. The conversation flowed and there never seemed to be any awkward silences. We connected intellectually as well as we had connected on the dance floor.

After our meal he smoothly managed to extend the evening by asking if I wanted to take a walk by the waterfront. He pulled me down onto a bench under a heavy, phosphorescent moon and commenced to kiss me. Perhaps he was nervous. Perhaps he was intimidated by an older, seemingly more experienced woman. Whatever the case, he was not kissing me well. I wrote him off right there under the stars.

He called me soon after to ask if he could see me again. I thought, why not? It was the first heat wave of the year and I offered him a cold beer and a run through the sprinkler, owing to my lack of a swimming pool. He gamely donned a pair of men's boxers that I often wore, which unfortunately were white. They were darn near see-through after a couple of charges through the water. He swiftly covered himself with a towel and took to drinking his beer. He still had not made much of an impression on me. I continued to see him for lack of a better offer.

The next time he called, I proposed a casual date and invited him to come watch me play softball. My only condition was that he baby-sit my three-year-old while I was at bat or on the field – over half the game. He agreed and I told him where and when to meet me. As I warmed up by passing the ball around with a couple of girls, I heard a motorcycle off in the distance and the din of the engine as it grew closer. His sports bike pulled up in the parking lot and Wayne dismounted, removed his helmet and strolled over to me. My palms got all sweaty and my knees weak as I finally took a good look at him. His jeans clung to him like a second skin contouring his thighs. He wore a turquoise, cotton, long-sleeved T-shirt that reflected his eyes and his hair was tumbling, loose and curly. I found I was unable to speak. Why had I not noticed how absolutely gorgeous he was?

To cover my sudden nervousness I brusquely told him to keep an eye on Matthew. He reassured me by saying, "I used to watch my ex-girlfriend's son all the time. Don't worry about us."

He strolled over to the bench and I eyed every step he took, as did most of the women on both teams. By the second inning I was beginning to relax and I noted with satisfaction that Wayne was following the game very closely. Except where was Matthew? I charged out of the dugout to find that my boy had wandered out into the street. He had just stepped off the curb and gave a yelp as I collared him. I marched him back to a stricken look-ing Wayne who was clambering off the stands and com-ing to meet us. I handed back my son, who did not even have the sense to look like he had done anything wrong, and gave them both a stern warning. "This had better not happen again."

Wayne nodded and gently took Matthew's hand. He managed to keep him sitting and/or nearby for the rest of the game. That was exactly how long it took me to cool off.

As I collected my gear and stowed my shin pads, Wayne came over with Matthew safely in tow and said, "How about I treat you both to an ice cream?"

We drove over to the ice cream parlour. Wayne chose chocolate, Matthew vanilla and I had coffee ice cream. We went outside to enjoy the late afternoon sun. I stood near the door and Wayne was about a foot away. He said bluntly, "You have great legs."

Wow.

"Thank you," was all I could gasp. His approach was not very subtle, but effective.

The next day, I did something that was highly out of character, but I had such a strong premonition that I did it anyway. I bought a dress, a really fancy party dress. It was black with a white bustier that was a large shiny bow. Maybe, for most, the purchase of a dress was nothing special, but as a single mother staying within my budget meant no new dresses, party or otherwise. My intuition proved correct shortly after, when Wayne telephoned to ask me to come with him to Toronto for his sister's wedding on July 1. I said I'd love to come, and that I had the perfect dress.

We drove in my car and stopped past the Ontario border to eat at a rest stop. I had packed a lunch of shrimp mousse sandwiches, my absolute favourite.

Wayne dutifully ate every bite with a flourish but months later warned me, "Never make that crap again." He was on his best courting behavior, for now.

We drove into Mississauga, a suburb of Toronto, and somehow found his sister Wanda's street. Toronto seemed to have so much less land than Montreal, the houses all seemed jammed together and had an endless sameness about them. Her particular house was on a corner lot and had a sweeping inlaid stone driveway. It was pink and new with a large foyer. Wayne's sister greeted me warmly with a hug and led us through the house out to the back where there were several people relaxing and taking a bit of sun. One man was reclining on a lawn chair. When he stood he had stripes of red and white on his excessive belly where rolls of fat had hidden the skin.

He introduced himself by saying, "I just quit smoking." He nodded and continued, "I went to a hypnotist and it works."

I told him that was great and looked for Wayne. He was sitting on a lounger with his sister and they were drinking something suspiciously wet and cold looking. Wanda's fiancé, Gary, introduced himself and offered me a drink, I mumbled an appropriate affirmative.

Armed with a refreshment, I joined the siblings. Wanda was glowing and had a smile even wider than Wayne's. They reminded me briefly of Donnie and Marie Osmond. The sun-stripy man came over and Wayne said, "This is my father Winston."

Wayne's dad tipped his baseball cap and the sun shone off his white dome. This man should not be out in the sun, I thought.

Gary showed us to our room so we could stow our gear. It was Wanda's sewing room and it was a good thing that it was carpeted, because we didn't have a bed. Owing to the huge number of guests sleeping over, we were lucky to have blankets and a door to close. Soon everyone was preparing for the rehearsal dinner and we left for the church and the restaurant. I was seated between Wayne and his mother Regina.

Regina was not overly tall, but with her dark hair and skin tone and her pugnacious manner, she was formidable. She was quite intoxicated with the excitement of her oldest daughter's nuptials, but I got the keen sense that Wayne bringing a girl to Toronto was something special as well. I was being furtively scrutinized, no mistaking that.

After dinner, we went back to our tiny room, closed the door, stretched out on the floor and naturally settled into a spoon embrace. My back curved into his front and he held me gently. I started to talk, silliness mostly, and he started to listen. I started to cry and he held me that way for over two hours. No one had ever held me like that before and no one had ever listened to me, ever.

I told him, "Nobody's ever spooned with me before."

"Really?" He seemed surprised.

I told him that I hadn't had much affection in the past and that this was all a bit overwhelming. Wayne rubbed my back in a non-suggestive manner and continued cuddling me until I feel asleep on his dead arm. Little did I know that he had endured an earful from his soon-to-be brother-in-law about how I hadn't yet put out and what was the problem? It seems that Wayne had a reputation with the ladies and that our unconsummated relationship was quite out of the ordinary for him. I slept blissfully unaware and awoke feeling better than a night on the floor warranted.

The next day was startlingly beautiful, with an arc of clear blue and a sun high in the sky by noon. The bride was deep in her preparations and I was fortunate enough to witness the ablutions. Her hair and makeup specialist was applying the finishing touches, which included jabbing at her immobile hair style, heaped high with blond curls on her head, and spraying a fixative everywhere from the chest up. Her hair would never blow or even move in the wind, even though there was no breeze and the heat was building outside. Nor would her makeup smudge, smear or run away. It seemed it would take a scraper to remove it, but she was stunning.

The ceremony was performed in a white clapboard chapel and the couple beamed happily from their stretch white limousine before they rode to their reception at a harbourfront hotel. We would be spending the night there also and rode with the wedding entourage to check in. We arrived at the Harbour Castle Hotel and were shown to our room. I took one look at the king-sized bed, at Wayne's king-sized grin and charged back down to the front desk.

"That room simply will not do," I said. "I want two queen size beds. There's been some kind of mistake."

The man behind the desk said that Wayne had specifically asked for a king.

"Well he doesn't want it anymore," I retorted. I fixed Wayne with a glare and within minutes we had a new room on another floor. We dumped our stuff and headed to the party.

I was in for many, many introductions as I soon learned that Wayne had a lot of relatives. I patiently shook hands with assorted aunts, uncles and cousins, certain I would forget most of their names. Uncle Yvon gripped my hand, and when I returned his shake in a firm manner, he approvingly said to Wayne, "She's got a real good grip my boy."

I blushed scarlet and he gave me a not so uncly kiss on the cheek. I guessed he was about ten years older than I was. Regina, Wayne's mom, was only fifteen years older.

After the meal came the drinking and the dancing. Wayne was sweating profusely from our exertions on the dance floor (frustrated sexual energy), and frequently returned to our table for a swig of his scotch. He took a swipe at his not so recently shaved face, and left bits of paper napkin peppered all over his stubble. I was giggling and grinding and having a great time. Gary called all the guests out to the balcony and said to Wanda, "I've arranged fireworks for you as a gift." She went all misty as the spectacle erupted for almost twenty minutes of extravagant explosions over the water. She cried at the finale and Gary took full credit for something that had been arranged and paid for by the Canada Day committee to celebrate Canada Day.

We had danced much of the alcohol out of our systems, but enough remained to make our way tipsily back to our room. I disrobed in the bathroom and put on a not-sexy-on-purpose nightgown. I crept back into our bedroom and sat on the edge of Wayne's bed. He was ready for anything under the blankets and was surely encouraged when I began to kiss him. A few minutes of rather steamy necking and I was unsure of which bed to climb into. Something caused me to hold back. I wasn't ready and I regretfully pulled away from his embrace. The gentleman kissed my nose and I crossed over to the dark side, away from his light, to sleep alone. The stage had been set though. He really had me all worked up and I had to cool off before I could nod off.

The drive home was a long, extended version of the night before, but without any kissing. It was July 2 and it was scorching. My little car was air conditioner deprived, and even with all the windows and the sunroof open, it was still hot. So was Wayne with his shirt off. His chest was covered nicely with man hair. He smelled of musk. He reached over and rubbed my knee. He alternated between my knee and just above my knee for six hours. It was an ordeal to stand up after all that stimulation. He kissed me, thanked me for a great weekend and went home.

He called later and asked if I wanted to go to La Ronde with him, my sister Lorraine and Paul. I agreed and my brother-in-law picked us up at my place the following Saturday.

Wayne wasn't much for the rides. He gallantly went on one with the rest of us that most closely resembles a salad spinner, the gizmo that removes water from the leaves by centrifugal force. In our case, we were plastered to the sides by the gravitational pull, and while Paul was crawling upside down like a lunatic spider, both Wayne and I struggled to keep a lid on it. I managed not to heave on the pavement once I was standing on terra firma and sucked in the fresh air like a fish floundering at the bottom of a boat. We begged off the rest of the evening, claiming a sudden attack of the flu, and Paul reluctantly drove us home. We wrestled in the back seat, kissed quite a bit and mysteriously my bra was removed. By the time we arrived it was quite late and I told Wayne he might as well sleep over.

"Where?" he asked.

"With me," was my flippant reply.

Wayne crawled into bed looking quite green, turned on his side and was asleep instantly. I gratefully slipped into my side of the bed and I slept well in that bed for the first time in a very long time. I was not alone.

The following morning, I cracked open an eyelid, glanced at the form beside me and hustled into the bathroom. I scrubbed, showered, shampooed and brushed everything that could be cleaned. I felt marvelous, alive. I wrapped myself in a pure, white towel. I wound another around my damp hair. I stepped into my bedroom and stood across the bed from a very wide-awake man.

"What do you want me to do with this towel?" I asked.

He didn't even take the time to answer before it was on the floor.

8

IT'S BEEN TWO
WEEKS, WHY HASN'T
HE MOVED IN?

Things changed after we finally did it. It became so that we could barely stop doing it. I felt as if he had become part of me and I was loath to see him leave to go home after each wonderful day. A positive indication that our relationship was moving forward came soon after. He invited me to dinner with his parents and he was going to cook.

His mother and father were already at Wayne's apartment when I arrived. They were enjoying a glass of wine. His mother was quick to say, "I am finally able to sleep at night since Wayne met you."

I answered that I really loved her son. Wayne's mother smiled and returned to her seat next to Winston.

Wayne was in the kitchen preparing the escargots in garlic that were a prelude to the steaks, fries and salad that followed. He was proving to be a good cook, definitely a bonus. I left happy but determined to find a way to make that man live with me. I was so focused on my plan that I got lost and took an extra hour to find my way home.

I invited Wayne over the next day and the morning sun rose with the promise of a superlative late July day. I donned a flowery frock and pulled my hair up off the base of my neck. Matthew had been sent to the ex-husband, an elaborate lunch lay in wait in the fridge. The stage was set. After we had eaten, we moved to the front porch to allow our meal to settle.

I asked Wayne if there was anything he wanted to tell me, in the hopes that he would blurt out how he really felt and say that he loved me.

"No," he replied.

I continued to press the matter. "I'm sure there must be something you want to say."

To which he answered, finally realizing what I was about, that he loved me. Whereupon I answered in kind and we kissed.

I felt wonderful and thrilled that I had helped him to express feelings that he had obviously bottled up, and was crushed to learn years later that he had been pushed into saying it just to keep from hurting me.

Now that we loved each other, my next project was to get him to move in. I begged God to force Wayne into shacking up and went around spouting inanities like, "Wouldn't it be great if we lived together" and "Too bad you have to drive so far away every night." I had about as much subtlety as a mallet. He was so not ready to live with a woman, but fate managed to find a way. After pestering him for a couple of weeks, he was evicted from his apartment. It had something to do with a flood and the fire department being dispatched to break down doors and stuff. He charmingly brought up the matter that night as we sat on the floor in the living room watching television.

"You know how you've been hinting that maybe I should move in? Well, I seem to be available and wondered if this weekend would be okay?"

I scrambled to my feet and pulled him up into my embrace. If he had any doubts at all about how I would react, they were banished. We made plans for the transition the following Saturday morning.

That weekend I eagerly awaited him and his friend Ray who were due to arrive with a car and trailer. I bounced down the drive after Ray backed in and rushed to meet Wayne's friend. He climbed out of the car, pulled open the hatch of the trailer and squatted on the tailgate. He was bulgy around the middle, greasy on top, and his hands shook. He seemed to be experiencing the DTs. But he had helped Wayne to pack, had driven everything over and Wayne seemed to really like him, so I was determined to like him too.

"Got any beer?" he mumbled as he fumbled to shove a cigarette between stained teeth.

"Get one for me too." Wayne asked.

I ran into the house to get a couple of cold ones.

The unpacking went quickly and Ray left soon after. Wayne emptied his few boxes and put away his clothes in the space I had cleared for him in the bedroom. I was over the moon with happiness.

I adjusted easily to the new routine and especially to having a *man* around the house. I made up a budget including his share of the mortgage payment and stuck it on the fridge with a running tab of any money that he borrowed or owed due to unexpected expenses. Wayne was not amused.

"What's this?" he asked one evening.

"It's just a way of keeping track of our finances."

"Yeah, well it doesn't belong on the fridge door."

At which point he tore down the list, crumpled it up into a ball and tossed it on the floor. I decided right there to keep tabs in my head, and as long as he paid his portion every month, we would manage.

I registered for university and began to study at Concordia that fall. Matthew was left with Wayne as I attended classes twice a week downtown. It was always a struggle to leave. I had no problem heading out the door except for a recently turned four-year-old standing in the front hall, holding tight to my leg and saying with a full pout on his lower lip, "Mommy, don't go to school."

I went anyway and forgot about everything as the joy of learning filled me up. I was taking a Psychology course. Emotional blackmail, from an inexperienced perpetrator at that, was not going to work.

One night, after a long session downtown, I returned drained and pushed open the front door of my darkened house. A light was on in the kitchen, and as I went to turn it off I noticed a piece of paper on the counter. It had a shiny globule on it and the words, "Honey, meet me upstairs," jotted around it. The drop on the paper was actually honey.

I dropped my book bag and headed to the stairs. I had to stop and read each note that had been lovingly placed on every step. Basically, Wayne was informing me how much he loved me and that he was waiting for me in bed. What was I waiting for? I wondered, and took the stairs two at a time. I checked Matthew, already knowing before I did that he would be gone for the night, in a sleep so deep and so different from his early days. I washed up in the bathroom and entered my – sorry, *our* – darkened bedroom. I took off my clothes and slid between the sheets to waken my slumbering man and do the things he had mentioned in the paper trail up the stairs.

Living together was about compromise, mostly on my part, but I'm sure Wayne had to make sacrifices too. When it all became too much for him, he relied on his safety valve to relieve the pressure. He would disappear.

The first time he did it I was frantic. He jumped on his motorcycle on a Friday after work and came back on Sunday. My entire weekend was spent watching from the window, never too far from the phone. Exhausted by late Sunday I could barely lift my head as his familiar exhaust rumble filled the air and preceded his return by about a minute. I ran out on the lawn and watched him disembark. He took off his helmet, lay it on the seat and pulled me to him. His rough whiskers scraped my cheek and his lips firmly drove home his meaning. He was back and he wanted me. No explanation was forthcoming, no apology, no words really, though I tried.

"Where were you?" I hollered for no good reason. "Why did you leave like that? Why didn't you call?"

Wayne shrugged his shoulders and rubbed his matted hair. "I had to get away. I needed some time by myself."

That was all the answer I was ever going to get. Wayne desperately required solitude and handled it in a haphazard, thoughtless way. This fella' was proving to be a complex mass of contradictory messages. He wanted me, but not all the time. He liked that I handled the money but he needed his independence. For the most part we fit together as neatly as the last two pieces of a beautiful puzzle. I was all about study, moderate drinking, staying home and healthy food. Wayne was party with your friends, ride your motorcycle long and hard, never eat breakfast, fall asleep in front of the television and don't go to the dentist unless it hurts. We were an odd pair.

His birthday was New Year's Eve and I was looking forward to our first celebration of it together. I called some of our friends and invited them to mark his twenty-fifth with a supper. They were all busy and I was very disappointed. On December 30, Wayne let me in on his plans.

"I'm going out with Terry and I don't know when I'll be back. We do this every year."

With that he was gone. He crawled in very early the next morning and slept until early afternoon. From then until the ball was dropped at midnight in Times Square, he lolled around the living room, alternatively on the couch or on the floor. He couldn't eat and barely drank water. He seemed quite ill.

Terry dropped by and laughed at his friend. "He gets like this every year, man," he said, slapping Wayne's pathetic foot perched on the arm of the sofa. "You should learn to handle it like me." With a smirk and a nod he left me with the smelly sack of potatoes that was my Wayne.

Matthew was growing and changing and a little while later he came to me to address a problem.

"Mommy, my toof is loose." He then proceeded to wiggle it with his fingers to illustrate, and for further proof he pushed on it with his tongue.

"Do you want me to pull it out?" I asked. I worked in a dentist's office and assumed Matthew thought I was actually some kind of dental professional.

"No, I want Wayne."

This surprised and pleased me, as it portended some type of bond developing between my two favourite males. I told him that Wayne wouldn't be back until later but I was sure he'd be happy to help. Matthew smiled, pushed on his tooth one more time for effect and literally skipped into the living room to watch television.

Wayne came home around six and grabbed a beer from the fridge. He kissed me and took a long drink after pulling back the tab. He slumped on the couch and said, "Man, I'm beat. I gotta find me another line of work." He was a skilled technician working at a paper company.

I began to explain about the tooth, but Matthew aborted my attempt by popping his head between us and wiggling his tooth at Wayne.

"Pull it out, Wayne."

Wayne looked at him with tenderness. "Give me a chance to take a shower and I'll do it then."

Matthew seemed more than satisfied and scampered back to his room. Wayne took his shower while I continued to prepare supper. Somewhere between dropping noodles in the water and sauteeing onions I peeked into the living room. Wayne was dressed in his underwear, sitting on the carpet with his legs spread. Matthew was kneeling between them facing Wayne with his mouth wide open and a look of complete faith on his face. Wayne had a Kleenex poised over the open maw as he moved in for the extraction. Not a word was spoken. Matthew blinked. Wayne reached in and pulled on the boy's front tooth. The paper tissue slipped off. He tried again with the same result. After multiple tries and nary a swear word, the deed was done. He handed Matthew the tooth and advised him to put it under his pillow. "The tooth fairy gives extra money for a first tooth."

Matthew carefully gathered the precious enamel and carried it in front of him like a last candle in a tunnel of darkness. As he passed me, he smiled his widest smile to reveal a glaring hole. He stuck his tongue in the space and dislodged the tissue still there to absorb any blood. I picked that up without him even noticing.

My work at the dentist's office had started out as an assistant's position that involved one month of on-the-job training with a woman who was going on maternity leave. Management soon discovered that my true talent lay in dealing with the clientele at the front desk and I became the receptionist. I enjoyed the work, filling in insurance forms, doing recalls and accounts receivable.

One day, a long-time patient was waiting patiently
while I filled in her claim form and somehow we began
discussing husbands. She was a vibrant, sensual woman
in her early fifties, with Latin features and dark thick
hair. Her husband, who was also a client, appeared to be
similarly fiery and explosive. As my situation with
Wayne was comfortable though unpredictable after a
couple of years, I wanted to talk about the long term. I
asked her how she had managed to stay married for so
long.

"We have passion," was her reply. But was it really as
simple as that?

"We fight big and makeup big," she said, "and after
almost thirty years, I'm grateful." Her husband joined
her at this moment, slipping a discreet hand around her
thickening waist to languish on her hip. She laughed and
leaned into him for a fraction of a second and that was
it. That was all I was going to see of their enduring, private love affair.

I had my own love to look after. Wayne was really the
one in this relationship who monitored its condition. He
would always be the one with his finger on the pulse of
our love. Whenever things seemed a little tense or we hit
a rough patch and I clammed up, he'd say, "What's up?"
or "Tell me what's wrong." He seemed to be continuous-
ly taking our couple's temperature and even the slightest
variation would lead to a time out and an investigation.
I was hesitant at the beginning to share my feelings,
because Mike hadn't even noticed me, let alone us, and
this attention was startling. With time I came to accept
and appreciate Wayne's caring ways. I was even able to

talk about how I felt and was pleasantly surprised when he listened. We didn't always work out every problem but the air would be cleared, which helped to eliminate some of the resentments. Some problems and differences remained entrenched, however, such as Wayne's cavalier attitude towards drinking. For him it was always a good time to have a beer. Or his inability to stick around when things got too hairy or he needed to think. But despite this, our core values and beliefs were quite similar. We loved each other with passion and managed to fall ever deeper in love.

I gave Wayne most of the credit for this, as he was supremely romantic. Just whispering in my ear as he caressed my face would cause me to go weak. Or he would look searchingly in my eyes and hold my hands and say, "I love you too much." He had this way about him. Did I mention his blue, blue eyes?

The summer of Matthew's sixth birthday, we planned a vacation to Gaspe. Mid-July is the only time one should even consider dipping more than a toe into the chilly water and this remains only the prerogative of tourists. Gaspesians don't swim. Even transplanted Gaspesians such as Wayne's parents don't know and don't care to know how to swim. That's for the codfish that are a main staple of the region. We drove north in one ten-hour-long stretch that included lunch in La Pocatiere and a pit stop in Murdochville. This town had been abandoned by the townspeople as the mining oper- ations had progressively shut down. A fire had cleared the forest and left a decimated landscape in its wake.

How desolate the terrain and how hopeless the feeling as we passed those empty houses and businesses.

Wayne's grandmother lived in a two-bedroom cottage overlooking the ocean. From the bluff beyond her front porch one could drop fifty feet and be dashed on the rocks below. Tall grass swayed in the perpetual breeze. I could taste the salt in the air and imagined how it was for this tiny French-speaking woman (she could only say "My God's sake" in English) to raise eight children in an ancient house that had only recently gained an indoor toilet. She had greeted us warmly and gathered Wayne to her full bosom at the first sight of him. She had auburn pin curls and round cheeks that threatened to close her brown eyes. They sparkled as she welcomed us with a big, "Bonjour."

We brought our luggage into the kitchen and Wayne dragged everything upstairs, where he was forced to stoop to enter the doorway of the bedroom that had housed his mother and her seven siblings. Wayne's paternal uncle Bernard had planned a family gathering for the following evening that promised fiddles, dancing and beer. I fell asleep after eating a four-and-a-half pound lobster, whose claws Wayne opened with a hammer. Wayne didn't have any of my crustacean due to over dosing on the beast during summertime childhood visits that saw him stuffing bits and pieces of the hated food between the cracks in the porch. When he was confronted by his mother, he said he had eaten his lobster, and showed her there was nothing left of his meal. She then asked what happened to the shell. To which he had no

answer, and was thereafter monitored during every feeding.

We went to the beach with Pamela and Randy, two of
Wayne's cousins, and had it to ourselves. The sun shone
and the temperature crept up to a sultry seventy. I lay
beside Wayne and watched Matthew splash in the small
waves. Wayne's cousins sat nearby, with Pamela playing
the guitar and softly singing country tunes into the wind.
I meanwhile methodically worked on manipulating
Wayne. I was determined that he would propose that
week. I asked him when he thought we should get married. Wayne choked on his beer.

"Are you serious?"

This was not the first time I had mentioned the dreaded "M" word, and until he asked me to marry him, it
would not be the last. His eyes scrolled the shoreline,
searching for an answer.

"Just let things happen naturally," was what he came
up with. He turned away from me, half buried his bottle
in the sand and closed his eyes. I stalked off, feigning
interest in the bushes growing haphazardly between the
rocks nearby. I dared him to follow or at least notice me.
He didn't. He dozed.

That evening we gathered at Uncle Bernard's for a
kitchen party. Wayne's deceased grandmother was a
famous fiddler and even had an annual trophy named in
her honour. Wayne's relatives on his father's side were all
talented musicians, and the fun had begun even before
we arrived. By eleven o'clock Wayne had drunk his fill
and we wandered outside, hand in hand. The moon was
almost full. The road sloped down to the ocean about

five hundred yards away. The surf roiled with a mythical rhythm as we started towards the shore.

Suddenly Wayne stopped me and said, "Will you marry me and be my wife? Will you grow old with me? Will you have my children and show them all the love that you show me?" He continued in this vein for a good twenty minutes, listing my attributes and repeating often and loudly that he loved me.

Well, that type of adulation is good for anyone's ego and I responded several times, "Yes." The moon and the ocean were a romantic backdrop for his proposal, but I would have agreed behind a Kentucky Fried Chicken outlet next to the trash bin.

We returned to the party and Wayne announced our engagement to his happy family. Since the proposal was so unexpected I had no ring, and though he was sincere, I discovered there would be no wedding either once Wayne sobered up. He simply never mentioned it again. After we had returned home, I eagerly bought bridal magazines and attempted to get him interested in picking a date and planning the celebration. He avoided commitment and I quickly dropped the subject and considered us unengaged. But what a lovely setting to which he had added his powerful words and swung me around and made my head spin. It remains the best proposal I have ever received, even though it came to naught.

The next couple of years were uneventful as we continued to adjust to each other's ways. Wayne remained an unpredictable enigma, a bad boy on a bike, and I liked it like that.

9

BREAKUP, MAKEUP, GET PREGNANT

It was spring, the lilacs were in bloom and I was in the Eastern Townships for the weekend visiting my parents. They lived in a log house planted on the side of a considerable mountain, one that took almost two hours to climb. My mother was outside working with bits of stained glass remnants from their studio and transforming them into a beautiful table with an abstract flower design. I sat next to her on a lounger and gazed out onto the sloping lawn that rolled down to their pond. I told her I wanted to have another baby.

"So have one," she said.

"But I can't, I'm not married."

"Yes, you can. You can always get married later."

Call my mother progressive, but I was stunned. I pondered what she said for a couple of weeks and decided to run it by Wayne.

I invited him to the same restaurant where we had had our first date. I had just gotten a raise and told him that I wanted to talk. That's code to a guy that something is really serious. We settled into our seats and I made an inane comment about the weather. Wayne fidgeted in his seat and kept glancing at his glass of wine to see if it was empty enough to fill. He wanted to know what this was all about.

We joked about our first date, when Wayne had gone into the kitchen instead of the bathroom. "That was on purpose," he said. "I wanted to meet the chef." He smiled at me and put his hand on mine. There's no better time to catch a trout than during a hatch so I seized the moment. I told Wayne that I wanted to have a baby and that we didn't have to be married to do it. He stared at me in amazement.

"When did you figure that out?"

I told him it was my mother who pointed out the obvious. He seemed unsure of what to do next.

"I guess we can talk about it."

"Wayne, we are talking about it. If you really love me you'll let me go off the pill and we'll see what happens. You're the one who always says we should let things happen naturally. Matthew is almost seven and we could dither over this for years. I want him to have a brother or a sister now."

Wayne looked uneasy and tried to make pleasant conversation for the remainder of the evening. We didn't discuss it further, which I took to be tacit approval of eliminating birth control from my daily routine.

What followed was definitely not routine. Wayne returned from work one day, completely sober, and told me he was leaving.

"I'm moving to Toronto," he said. "I'm starting a new life. I have to go see what's out there for me."

He packed some things upstairs and moved out. I could only stand and stare and watch his back as he pulled away. All during my divorce proceedings from Mike I could imagine us apart – heck, even before we married I could see us apart. But this I couldn't imagine. Even with my ability to picture almost anything, I just could not fathom us not a being a couple, a unit. I completely fell to pieces.

He didn't get as far as Toronto, but he did move back to Rosemere to stay with a friend. A few days after his departure he called and asked if he could come over. It was early evening when he pulled into my driveway. I was waiting on the front stoop. He entered the house behind me and we went into the living room. He dropped onto the sofa and I studied him. He was disheveled, with a white shirt and a scruffy chin. He looked like he had been drinking and was slightly hung over. To me he looked absolutely heavenly. I held myself back from sitting too close to him, in case I grabbed him and didn't let go.

"I miss you Karen." Wayne always had an ability to say things in a succinct yet thorough way.

"I really miss you too."

I didn't say anything about coming back or what he had been doing. I was determined to let him do the talking. We didn't talk much. Somehow, and rather quickly, we ended upstairs in bed having sex, really great sex. He left afterwards. He didn't discuss staying the night or what he was planning about us or that I was no longer on the pill. I naively assumed that he understood that I had gone off it, as well as the risks of pregnancy. He left and I didn't know when or if I would see him again.

The following morning I went to the dental clinic and, like everyday since the breakup, I had no appetite. I sat in the little kitchen in the rear of the office and looked around. The walls were white with bits of tape from long ago pictures that no longer hung there. The sink had three glasses containing old dishwater from the previous week. The floor had cracks and chips in the linoleum where the wooden folding chairs had scrapped repeatedly over the years. My lunch looked at me and appeared stale and unappealing. I rooted in the cupboard and found a box of saltine crackers. I took one and forced it into an unwilling mouth and down to a rebellious stomach. That became all I could manage for the next three weeks. One cracker a day didn't seem much for a person who had always eaten healthily and maintained a somewhat elevated weight.

Something was missing. The colour had gone out of my world. With Wayne gone, all that was left was black and white and it was bleak indeed. I was unable to enjoy my child, food, music, the wonderful sights around me. I could no longer appreciate life. He had somehow added dimension to my already good existence and made it great. He allowed me to experience and feel like never before. My life had been well worth living before I met him; he made it fantastic.

I became determined to win him back. I went over to my sister's house with a pregnancy kit. Her husband Paul was there, and as I put the box on the table, I told them I was late and might be pregnant. Paul, who was still good friends with Wayne, said that Wayne would have to come back if I was, since he was a decent guy. My sister actually shrieked and grabbed my shoulders.

The minute Paul went outside I told her the truth. "I'm not pregnant, but I want Wayne to think I am so that he stops being stupid and comes back home."

"But what are you going to do when he finds out that you are not pregnant?" She had a legitimate point, but I was fixated on the immediate solution and not the long-term repercussions of my scheme. I went in the bathroom and exited ten minutes later to an audience of two.

"I'm pregnant," I announced in a discouraged and hopefully believable voice. Lorraine tried to act happy for me and Paul was supportive

"He'll do the right thing," he said as he rubbed my arm. I was a con.

I telephoned Wayne when I got home and told him the news. He was silent for a long moment before he answered. I knew he would need time to absorb the ramifications of what I had just revealed to him and got off the phone with an "I love you." There was no reciprocal answer, besides, "Good bye."

Two days passed without a word. I was still unable to eat anything and had actually lost some weight – only two pounds, though. After not eating for three weeks you'd think that I'd have better results, and I'm not suggesting starvation as a diet tool. I took Matthew to visit my parents and was returning to the West Island via Autoroute 20, which was under construction. As traffic slowed on the raised down ramp I was forced to stop suddenly. Which I did very badly and hit the car in front of me. Matthew was perched behind me with his seatbelt on when I crashed and bashed his cheekbone, near his eye, into the headrest. The man I hit was ever so kind and considerate, considering that I could have avoided the collision by being more alert and stopping behind him instead of in his trunk. An ambulance and tow truck appeared at the same time. Matthew was treated for a small cut that had appeared and was trickling blood. Then we transferred to the tow truck with my nifty Nissan Sentra dragging its tail in the rear.

I called Wayne and told him about the car accident and that I thought I was having a miscarriage. Lying felt terrible. I am usually a completely honest woman and I had no excuse for my deceit. I had gotten my period that morning and was convinced that this would extricate me from my lie of a few days before. Wayne came over as soon as he could and was wonderfully solicitous. He told me to rest and that he'd take care of Matthew. He wasn't up to asking any details about how I knew I was miscarrying, but we did talk about the accident. Somehow it seemed to be a fortuitous event. At the very least, it had brought Wayne to me and he seemed very concerned. He began coming over every day.

His visits were sometimes brief, but other times they would extend into the morning. It felt natural to have him there when I woke up. He would lie there with his eyes open, usually gazing at me as the light filtered its way into my consciousness. He would hold me and love me. Normally, I would have tried to manipulate his feelings towards my end, but I somehow remained separate and serene. I was content just to have him there and dared not breathe for fear that he would escape.

He called me a few days later on Canada Day. It was the anniversary of our trip to his sister's wedding in Toronto and we had adopted it as our own special day. He invited me to meet him at Cheers, a local bar. I asked my friend Myrna to come with me in case I was about to receive bad news. I sat down with a cooler to wait. It was smoky and loud with laughter and talk. The light was dim and I could smell the spicy chicken wings being prepared for Happy Hour. We waited for over an hour before Wayne dragged himself through the door.

"You're not the only one crashing," he said. "I hit the curb on the exit from the highway and dropped the bike in the grass. Luckily, it only got scratched."

"What about you?" I asked, trying not to let my frenzy show.

He said he was fine. But isn't that what he always said? Besides a broken something, he'd have to be comatose and unable to resist before he'd go to a doctor.

He sat on the empty stool next to me and signaled for a beer. The attractive barmaid rushed over with a cold one. I made nervous small talk with Myrna while he took a few sips and drags of his cigarette.

He gave me a nudge and asked, "Do you still want to try?"

My only response was to kiss him. Myrna chuckled, patted Wayne on the shoulder, and sensing a reunion, departed for home. We left soon after, meeting back at the little semi-detached on Roundtree Crescent.

Wayne had come home and I was supremely grateful. Three days later, I made the pilgrimage to St. Joseph's Oratory in Montreal. I was sorry for lying, but bypassed the hundreds of wooden stairs out front that worshippers frequently crawl up, praying on their knees. I walked from the parking lot and found myself in a chapel off from the great hall. I settled in a pew near the back and relaxed in the serene atmosphere. The ceiling must have been over fifty feet high. The exterior wall had large, arched stained glass windows, the portraits of saints. Since I was not a regular at church, not even an irregular, I only recognized Jesus on the cross at the front. I was practically alone except for a couple of older ladies fervently praying in the front row.

A voice spoke to me. It said, "You are pregnant." It came not in a direct, in-your-ear manner but in a vibrational, soundless way. It came not from any particular direction but found its way into my head. It seemed feminine but not overtly so. I snickered. I looked around me, all the way around, front and back. I was by myself. I felt warm and safe and very confused. The idea of doing a pregnancy test popped into my head. I said a prayer of gratitude for the return of Wayne and dashed out.

I purchased a test kit and went home to use it, even though I was not late and had no other indications that I might be pregnant. I even knew that pregnancy tests are much more accurate after actually having missed a period.

Since this time I was really going to open the pregnancy test box, that meant that I would have to read the instructions. They included gems like, "Allow the stream of urine to run on the test wand." Wand doused and in hand, I sat on the toilet seat cover and waited for a positive or a negative indication. Ever so slowly a positive result appeared. Even though I knew there was always a chance of having a false positive, I was certain that it was positively not false. I was finally, amazingly pregnant. Now, to tell the unexpecting father.

The month before, when I had told him the same news, it was by telephone, it had been a lie and we were separated. Happily, on this occasion we were once again together and I was going to share the news face to face. He came home from work and we met in the kitchen, next to the refrigerator. He kissed me heartily as was his way and opened the door of the fridge so that he could have a beer. While he was rooting about I announced from the other side of the door that we were going to have a baby. He closed the door and with both empty hands pounded the wall.

"Are you sure?" he asked.

I told him I was. He looked at me with dark, troubled eyes.

"I'm going away for a few days. I'm not sure when I'll be back."

He padded upstairs and packed his backpack. He came back down and kissed me well and left me. He floored his motorcycle after backing out of the drive and without stopping at the stop sign, he rounded the turn and roared away. The vibration of the departing engine and resounding whine of metal and combustion eventually faded. I dropped to the cement steps before my house. My knees were weak and my stomach was ready to empty its few contents in the bed of tiger lillies. The flowers nodded their orange heads at me. They agreed that Wayne was impossible.

He called the next day. His voice quavered as he spoke.

"I'm going to Gaspé with some buddies. I gotta think this through. It has nothing to do with how I feel about you, that will never change, I love you to death."

He hung up and I prepared to wait, however long it took. Fortunately he came back less than a week later. I was not expecting him and as usual my head lifted when I heard the familiar sound of the Kawasaki engine. He was dirty and his hair was plastered to his head. He hugged me and held me close for a long while. He smelled of sweat and engine oil. He pulled his pack from the front of the bike where it had been strapped for many hundreds of miles and trudged into the house. I followed him in and up the stairs. He dropped his things on the floor and slowly stripped his muddy clothes. He asked me to run him a hot bath.

He stepped in before it was half full and sank his weary body in the steamy water. I sat on the toilet seat and contemplated his face. His eyes were shut and sweat was beginning to form on his forehead.

"I'm so fucking tired. It rained for ten hours straight. Hard, driving rain. We could barely see the road." He leaned right back and sank further into the tub. His arms were on the sides and I noted the raised veins on his muscles. He opened his eyes. They were enveloped by red rims and tears stood poised. "What kind of a father am I going to be?"

I had no answer to give him.

"My father wasn't much of an example, I don't know if I can do this," he said.

I had seen Wayne with Matthew, I had watched him care for and love my son. I was at school two evenings a week and Wayne never minded baby-sitting. He was so good, I knew he was as ready as he'd ever be.

"I know you'll be a great father. All the love in you will have a new person to be lavished on."

I left him to soak and ponder in peace. He did have eight months to get used to everything.

I quickly began to gain weight. With Matthew I had carefully monitored my food, walked five miles a day, gone swimming and to the gym, and even played tennis. And yet I had gained about sixty pounds. With this pregnancy, I once again was watching what I ate and exercised regularly, but I seemed to be heading to the same Sumo weight class, only faster.

In early October, Wayne and I went for the baby's first ultrasound at the Lakeshore General Hospital. I drank twenty-four ounces of water two hours before the procedure, as directed. It was way too much. The ultrasound technician at the hospital explained that my kidney function was so good due to my drinking vast quantities of water regularly, that I could have managed on half that, one hour before. She told me to urinate, but not all of it.

Imagine that, having to pee so very badly and only being allowed to do so halfway. That's the real water torture. I dutifully stopped even though I was bursting to continue and returned to the examining room to lie down. She squirted the gel on my belly, rolled the device over my stomach and told me to do it again. She still couldn't see properly.

The first time was bad. The second time, trying to stop the flow was painful. I waddled back and flopped on the examining table. The technician managed to complete the procedure and informed us that we would have results at our next visit with Dr. Hayden.

Sometimes I was very excited about the baby and other times, not so. Wayne seemed to be under tremendous pressure and was worried about everything. It appeared that he took fatherhood way more seriously than step-fatherhood.

We went with my sister, Lorraine, to look at a new house in Pierrefonds. We had decided that a two-bedroom cottage was not suitable for a family of four. The new house was a three-bedroom bungalow with a finished basement and a beautiful stone fireplace. While we were having tea with the owners, I felt so at home and so comfortable that when Wayne asked for a teaspoon, I jumped up before the owner could move and fetched the spoon from the correct drawer. We put in an offer that night and it was accepted.

Now we had to sell our house. Wayne painted the living room to make it more saleable and we both set about trying to fix up the house in our own way. I kept it as neat and tidy as possible and Wayne was doing all the small repairs that he had never had time for before.

"I'm glad that we're finally getting our own house," he said one day as he was raking the leaves.

"What do you mean? This place is yours too."

"Not really. My name isn't on anything. This will be my first house."

He raked more purposefully after that statement and I understood that he was really excited. It was nice.

Wayne took me to a Montreal Canadien's hockey game with his sister, Wendy, and her boyfriend, Pierre. The excitement in the old Forum was palpable and I believe it transferred to the baby. It did a complete flip while I was trying to get comfortable in my wooden seat. The players surged onto the ice and I was once again impressed with just how large they appeared wearing skates and up close. The action played from end to end and the hockey players hammered each other continually with checks. My back was aching the entire evening and my hips hurt so much that you would have thought I had been playing.

I got an emergency telephone call two days later from the school secretary, who said that Matthew had fallen. My heart was pounding because no call from the school can be good news. I asked how bad it was and if I should come from work.

"No, he seems okay," she said. "He's sitting here by my desk."

I relaxed and told her I would come later in the afternoon when I finished work. I was not expecting anything serious, so I had quite a shock when I saw

Matthew's little face. His lip was gashed and bleeding and definitely going to need stitches. His face was swollen and both, BOTH, front teeth were broken! He had been sitting in the same chair for more than four hours, his facecloth was blood-soaked and the ice had long since melted. With large brown eyes that had long ago ceased crying, he looked at me and asked what took so long.

I turned to the secretary.

"Why didn't you tell me his teeth were broken? He's going to need stitches." I stared at her with my anger barely contained.

"Well, I don't know what he looked like before," she answered.

I grabbed Matthew by the hand and led him out to the car. He recounted how a bigger boy from grade four pushed him. My big belly and I squeezed behind the wheel and prepared to head back downtown into the severe traffic of rush hour, because the Montreal Children's Hospital was the best in town. The Lakeshore General Hospital was, to my mind, only for having babies. The emergency trauma unit at the Montreal Children's Hospital was the place for us.

Matthew didn't have much to say but he was scared. He became even more frightened when, after a short wait in emergency, they shuffled us into a treatment room. Matthew's lip was frozen and he received five stitches. The doctor said we'd have to go to a dentist for the rest of the work.

My boss, Dr. Jay Waxman would take care of that for me. He saw Matthew the following Saturday and ground down slightly his two front adult teeth. He did such a marvelous job that I could hardly tell that Matthew had had an accident.

We continued cleaning and painting. The real estate agent came to put the house on the market. I worked so hard that I could barely walk. I also managed to electrocute myself and after visiting the medical clinic, I was even more concerned. They had been unable to find a fetal heartbeat. My obstetrician found it quickly enough at my next checkup, because, I'm sure, his equipment was more sophisticated and suited to monitoring a fetus.

I gained another nine pounds. I had two blood tests and a diabetes test. My second ultrasound followed in the middle of January and Wayne wouldn't let me find out the sex of the baby. He said he wanted it to be a surprise. Well, I didn't want a surprise this time and asked the technician.

"I think it's a girl," he said. "I don't see anything between her legs."

We walked down the hallway towards the front of the hospital and the parking lot, and I asked Wayne to go on ahead and get the car warmed up. He kissed me and left.

I stopped at the hospital chapel. A few flickering votive candles gave a welcoming glow. I settled in the front pew and asked that this child of mine be born healthy, that he would not have any of the terrible problems that I had had to deal with with Matthew. It felt like a moment of understanding, almost as if I had a premonition of what was to be. I felt the weight of caring for my unborn child heavy on my shoulders.

Even though the house was officially on the market, Wayne decided to decorate the baby's room. Matthew was moved into the basement, two floors down. I was very uncomfortable with that arrangement, as he was still young enough to occasionally need a mother in the middle of the night for whatever reason, be it illness or a scary dream. Matthew didn't seem to mind; boys are so different from girls. When I was young and four years older that he was, my parents moved me to the basement so that I could have a room of my own. I checked under my bed every night before I went to sleep and was never happy about being alone in the dark down there. He was thrilled.

Wayne went wallpaper shopping, and paint shopping, and door-knob and picture frame and mobile shopping. He came home with a whole zoo's worth of animals on a border consisting of every pastel colour known to expectant fathers. He lavished paint on the wall far into the night and bordered with the best. His true calling seemed to be interior design, because when he was done, it was a masterpiece, including the mint coloured knobs and Winnie the Pooh lamp. I clapped upon seeing the finished room.

"You could send a picture of this to a magazine," I said. "It's fantastic."

Wayne pulled me to him and embraced me, though his attempt at putting both arms around me failed due to my girth. The snow continued to fall outside. We had received fifteen inches already and expected more. I contentedly snuggled closer to Wayne and laid my head on his shoulder. I took a deep breath and thought about the baby that was going to live in that bedroom and whose arrival was only one month away. I felt ready.

My mother-in-law decided I needed a baby shower and I was surprised with one that weekend. I was wearing an unfortunately coloured, bright orange sweatsuit, and looked like a rotund pumpkin. Wayne knew about the party and could have advised me to change, especially since he hated that outfit. The weather was again stormy and some of the guests cancelled. The stalwarts that showed included my hung-over sister, my cousin Nancy, Wayne's younger sister, Wendy, (his older sister Wanda had just given birth to a little girl in Toronto), my mother, some of Wayne's aunts and his mother's friends and Myrna. I was made to put a cardboard plate on my head covered with bows, though I must admit that I did enjoy all the silliness. I received every manner of sleeper and baby-care paraphernalia, including a sturdy car seat. Now I was really ready.

The morning of Sunday, March 8, found me with back and stomach cramps. I had had my first child by cesarean section after my water broke. I was no expert on labour, real or false. I went to the hospital to find out if it was time and the doctor ordered a non-stress test. I was hooked up to a machine and waited a few hours. The results must have been a go, because they admitted me. Wayne went to buy champagne, but they released me at six that evening and told me to come back on Wednesday. I went home very discouraged and very tired.

On Wednesday, I showed up promptly at nine in the morning, fully expecting to have a baby that day. I came out of the bathroom and bumped into my former broth-er-in-law, Chris. I asked him what he was doing there and he said that he had just had a baby girl. He was hav-ing trouble articulating due to his feet not touching the ground. I managed to extract further information from the ecstatic new dad: his wife, Martha, was fine, the baby's name was Heather and everyone was well. This meant that Matthew was a cousin. Now, if only I could implore my baby to make an appearance, we could turn Matthew into a brother as well. No such luck, since the tests again were negative and I was sent home a failure. My baby was never going to be born and I would just be this fat lady with an alien living in my belly forever.

The baby had other ideas. We would be meeting very soon.

10
BABY MAKES TWO
SICK KIDS

"Have you noticed how much snow has fallen?" I asked innocently. Normally so much snow in March would really up the cabin fever quotient, but being ready to give birth any minute had left me with the urge to nest. I was cocooning on a Friday night and we were watching skating on TV. I loved being pregnant; Wayne let me watch stuff he abhors.

I started to feel cramping in my belly. I waited and about ten minutes later I felt it again. The pain was very mild, but since I was due in four days, I told Wayne I thought I might be having labour pains. His eyes took on the glazed fear of a raccoon caught in the headlights of a Mack truck.

Hoping that it was just gas or false labour, I settled back into my cozy couch and watched the lithe skater jump and twirl her little heart out. An hour passed and though the cramps continued, they neither varied in tempo nor increased in intensity. I was very unsure of what to do next and, upon inspection of the weather situation outside, was rather worried about the storm that was dumping tons of snow.

I called my mother and she told me to go to the hospital immediately, since the snow was making the roads dangerous and they were becoming impassable. That made good sense and I should have listened, but how sensible was I at forty weeks gestation? I was happy to continue watching the skating on TV.

Wayne grabbed the phone and said, "Don't worry Irma, I'm taking her." He hung up and called my brother-in-law, Paul, and asked him to meet us at the hospital to pickup Matthew. There was no dilly-dallying, no question that Wayne was in charge, and I was happy to let him do the thinking. My attention moved inward, towards the baby that was most likely making its way into the world.

As I struggled to put on my boots, Matthew asked if he could help. He gave me a sleepy smile. He suddenly appeared taller and infinitely more mature.

We piled into my car and Wayne backed out of the driveway. And that's where we stopped. The car would not budge. It was stuck in a four-foot snow bank at the end of the driveway. We left the car half on the road and struggled through the snow to our neighbour's house across the street. Dan came to the door and didn't hesitate to drive us to the hospital in his four-wheel-drive pickup truck. He would later dig out our car and shovel the driveway while we were away.

The city was deserted. There were absolutely no cars on the roads and most were impassable. We managed to find a circuitous route to the front entrance of the hospital and were met by the incredibly clever Paul. He seemed to have had no trouble getting there and brought Matthew safely back home.

Wayne guided me to the maternity floor. I was led to the labour room and gratefully laid down. The pains were still coming approximately ten minutes apart and were not quite as subtle as they had been. After being examined by Celeste, my nurse, I learned that I was indeed in labour. A fetal heart monitor was strapped to my swollen mid-section and I listened to the galloping of my child's heart. With hourly checks by the nurse, we managed to get through the night without change in my condition. Wayne dozed on the vinyl chair in the corner, waking every so often in a fit of snoring, to inquire how I was doing. Whereupon he would rapidly succumb and I would watch his sleeping form. He was as excited as he was exhausted and needed the sleep. I managed a few fifteen-minute catnaps and felt ready to tackle the world. My body was geared up for the grueling event ahead.

By mid-afternoon of the following day, Dr. Hayden decided to speed things along with an induction, after yet another inspection revealed that nothing had changed.

The induction consisted of an IV drip containing oxytocyn and in breaking the watery sack in the uterus housing the baby, which was done with a hooked knitting needle type instrument. Once the doctor had inserted the instrument and supposedly broken my water (a painless procedure) there was not a drop to be seen. The doctor pried, poked and punctured again with the same result.

Without explanation, the doctor announced that it was going to be a dry birth. Not to worry dear, just the dry facts. I wished then that he had been a she, one who had given birth to a dozen babies, all at the same time. Since Matthew had been a C-section, having a vaginal birth on my second go round was termed a VBAC, meaning a vaginal birth after Caesarian. Having no water to facilitate the delivery was sure to make things extremely difficult.

The drip seemed to be doing its magic as my pain was increasing exponentially and the contractions had sped up considerably. Natural labour progression is usually slow and steady and conceivably allows the mother to adjust to the increasing demands placed on her coping mechanism. Induction skips the transition step and goes from zero to full-blown labour in what seemed to me like sixty seconds. I was not prepared for the sudden, incredible pain. I tried to cope for as long as I could, but after a couple of hours I told Wayne to get me an epidural. I was unable to gather strength between contractions because they were coming so fast and furious that there was no time. I had reached five centimetres of dilation. Wayne quickly fetched the doctor who gave me an epidural. The minute the needle was in my spine, I relaxed. I perked up immediately. Wayne was also relieved. He couldn't stand to see me in so much pain.

Upon further examination, my cervix was a lovely ten centimetres. Let the games begin. I was brought into the delivery room, a steely cold place with drab green paint and stainless steel everywhere. My world became very small. In the periphery floated the obstetrician and Wayne. My breathing became very concentrated and I was tuned to the doctor's every word. When he told me to push, I pushed. But it didn't seem to be enough. Even though I was pushing, the baby was not coming. Dr. Hayden said that I had better have him on the next push, or he would have to use forceps. From what I knew, forceps were not a baby-friendly tool. I feared for my child and when the next contraction hit and I was ordered to push, I did. With every fiber and muscle of my being I forced that baby out of my belly, down the birth canal and out. In doing so, I tore my perineum on both ends from my anus to my vagina. This type of ripping was known in the biz as a *fourth degree tear*. If not repaired properly, it can cause years of problems for the mother, which I found out the hard way.

I felt like I had moved a mountain with my vagina. My baby's head crowned and with the next few efforts I managed to push my second son out into the world and the waiting hands of my baby-catcher, Dr. Hayden. Further excitement awaited me when the doctor said it was a boy. I leaned into Wayne and absorbed his joy. He was enraptured by our son. Once the baby had taken his first breaths, he was placed on me for a few moments so we could appreciate what we had both accomplished. It is a magical, mystical journey when the bump on your belly grows into an actual living, breathing, thinking fellow human being. He was alert and looked at me with calm, studious eyes. My coach restrained himself from jumping and doing cartwheels and had to settle for holding his newborn and gazing at the perfection he had helped produce. The bonding had begun.

After the doctor finished the episiotomy, I was transferred to a room in the postnatal ward. I wanted to sleep, but my in-laws had managed to make it to the hospital through the snow, and I didn't want to disappoint them. Winston and Regina came to see me after looking in on the baby in the nursery.

"He's beautiful, a little angel," Regina gushed.

Winston was not quite so effusive, but was equally pleased, even though hospitals made him jittery.

"He's a Rooney alright. He's watching everybody in the nursery."

They left and Wayne made his departure soon after. He kissed me soundly on the lips and told me he loved me.

I was alone, except for the mother next to me who was keeping her curtain closed. I had heard her on the phone earlier and seen her baby. He had a clubfoot. I felt so sorry for her that her baby was not perfect. I remembered how that felt. I was thrilled that my baby was fine and had scored well on his Apgar tests. He was a healthy newborn, or so I believed.

I slept well until I heard the chorus of wailing that precedes the baby brigade. The babies are transported to their mothers for each feeding via a multi-level, wheeled vehicle and deposited in the correct waiting arms after identification is verified according to matching wristbands. Kyle Napoleon Rooney was handed to me after I moved to an armchair by the window and placed an inflatable rubber doughnut under my rear. He had a woven cotton hat with a rubber band closure. He was hungry and his mouth was open, awaiting a nipple. He was so familiar and yet a stranger. His first name was courtesy of his father, who was given the privilege of naming his son by virtue of the child being a boy. I selected his middle name based on both of our grandfathers's names and Wayne and Winston's middle name.

I fumbled with the two frontal slits in my new breastfeeding nightgown and soon produced a breast. Kyle rooted about for a moment before latching on to the nipple. He had a vigorous suck and I could feel my uterus contract with each pull. He also had a very familiar newborn smell that reminded me of his brother from the moment I held him. It was a fleeting fragrance that changed within days of his birth.

A nurse came in to offer assistance with nursing. When I put Kyle's head on my shoulder to burp him, she offered to show me another position. She took Kyle and sat him on her lap facing to her left. While holding his chin between her thumb and index finger, she alternately massaged and patted his back. He erupted contentedly, and she returned him to me to try the other breast. I was impressed. She moved on to the woman in the next bed and I returned my attention to Kyle.

He was beautiful. His skin was translucent, which by its paleness, made his dark hair appear even more so. His eyes were blue like all newborns's, but a smoky, intense blue that promised to turn to brown or hazel with time. He was docile and had yet to cry. I was sure I had the best baby in the world. He was returned to the attendant and all the babies were rolled back for a much quieter ride to the nursery. I dozed until I heard the breakfast trays being banged around in the hallway and was instantly alert. They were bringing me food. I looked out the window and was dazzled by the sight. The sky was an impenetrable blue and everything else was white. The sun shone brilliantly and its light was reflected off the astonishing amount of snow that lay everywhere, covering everything. All the dirt, slush and blemishes of the outside world had been eradicated. I wanted to feel the same way: fresh. I desperately desired a washcloth. I felt sweaty and like yesterday's gym socks.

I found the showers and entered a little room. I stepped under the spray. After fiddling with the control and managing to get a steady flow without scalding myself, my afterbirth smells mingled with the clean smell of disinfectant. It was exactly as I remembered it after having Matthew. I relaxed completely under the spray of the water-needles. Hot darts peppered my flabby body. Soap swirled and ran under my arms and down my legs. I purposefully lathered my scalp with too much shampoo and took forever to rinse it all away. I felt scrubbed and clean and finally alone in my body.

The movement in my belly had ceased. Its export reposed safely in the nursery under the supervision of some highly trained baby pros. I sauntered back to my room and began rooting for my hair dryer. The telephone rang. It was my mother, who said she'd be by later that afternoon after they'd shovelled out from under all the snow. We were chatting amiably when a woman came and stood at the end of my bed.

"Hang on a sec Mom, there's someone here to see me."

"I think you better call them back," the woman said.

I didn't hesitate after I'd caught the look in her eyes. My spine became a rigid pole and it took a supreme effort just to hang up the telephone and turn towards the stranger. She identified herself as the staff pediatrician and told me the chilling news.

"We've noticed that your son turns blue around the mouth when he cries. He'll have to go to the children's hospital for further tests. We know that he has a murmur, but we are unsure what else he might have. The very worst it could be is tricuspid atresia."

Where had I heard those words, *the very worst it could be*, before?

The pediatrician left shortly thereafter. There wasn't anything for me to say and she had no other information. I looked over at the woman and baby in the next bed packing up to go home and wished at that moment that all my son had was a club foot. At least I had had almost twenty-four hours of not knowing. I was grateful for that.

My little bubble of peace was shattered. I called Wayne in a panic and he came rushing over. He needed to hold his baby. We called my parents and they shoveled even faster so that they could make it in to the city. The rest of the day rushed by in a blur. It was a montage of crying and feeding and mourning the loss of my baby's health. My mother and father brought Matthew to meet his brother, a bittersweet occasion.

Wayne sat on the bed tenderly cradling Kyle. He wore a blue hospital gown over his jeans and turtleneck, his cowboy boots stretched out on my bed. Matthew leaned into him and gazed at his brother with a look of mingled awe and devotion. My parents beamed from the other side of the bed and I watched the entire circus from the corner of my room. I took pictures and murmured polite responses to everyone's effusive praise. My world had taken on a more sinister tinge. The light outside seemed somehow less pure.

The following morning I was introduced to two ambulance technicians who were to transport Kyle to the children's hospital. They had a steel chamber between them that was about three feet long and oblong in shape. It was similar to a cat-carrying case, but it was for my baby. Will he be able to breathe in that thing? I wondered.

While the technicians waited, I fed Kyle and Wayne packed our clothes and diapers. They took Kyle and put him in the portable iron lung. We stood there helplessly as he was rolled out the door. Nurses stood by, wordlessly watching him disappear. An older, white-haired nurse hugged me. It was upsetting for everyone when a newborn was sick, or even worse, died.

I dressed hurriedly and Wayne and I followed after our son. He was loaded into the ambulance and we tried to keep up. But somewhere on our way from the West Island to downtown we lost them. We were pulled over by the police near the Montreal Children's Hospital just off Atwater Street. The officer stopped in front of our parked car and walked back to our vehicle. I dragged myself out and hunched over the rear bumper. The policeman asked Wayne what was wrong.

"We're following our baby's ambulance to the hospital. My wife just gave birth, she's very upset."

The policeman offered to escort us to the hospital. I got back in the car and with the police car's lights flashing and siren blaring we made our way to Kyle. We weren't given a ticket for speeding.

We found Kyle and stood by his incubator where he was receiving oxygen. He slept and we worried. We attempted to cope with the unthinkable. After having already experienced the trauma of having a sick baby, I once again was facing something very familiar. Yet it was new and different at the same time. Kyle was not Matthew and we had no idea what lay ahead.

Kyle was whisked away for over three hours of tests: X-rays, an ECG and a special ultrasound for the heart. After he was fed, we met the cardiologist, Dr. Jutras.

The doctor led us into a small conference room and drew a picture of a heart. It was a skillful rendition.

"That's a normal heart," he said.

Then he proceeded to construct another image that looked like a warped version of the preceding heart.

"This is your son's heart."

I couldn't breathe. Kyle's heart didn't look like it could function; whole pieces of it were missing.

"Kyle has tricuspid atresia with a septal ventrical defect. He has a hole in his heart, which is the only reason he is alive. The blood flows in one chamber and back out the same way due to a missing valve."

Dr. Jutras continued to explain, in an oddly clinical manner, that since Kyle's vital signs were so good, they would wait until ten weeks to put in a catheter, six months to put in a shunt, and until he was two years old to perform the Fontan procedure. My baby was two days old and they were already planning three operations.

Dr. Jutras was probably more comfortable with children than with adults, so I tried to save my breakdown until after the interview. As I was also in considerable physical discomfort, I asked him to prescribe some pain medication. I'd suffered a bad tear during the birth and couldn't even sit down. He scribbled something on his prescription pad and Wayne and I went to the mall across the way to fill it. Seven years later and not much had changed, except for the man who was with me.

Various friends and family members came to visit during the five days Kyle spent in the hospital. They came to offer support, they came to sit and hold him, they came because they didn't know what else to do. Wayne and I tried to eat and sleep, but it seemed nearly impossible to do either. He was overwhelmed by his instant attachment to his son and the pain of having that joy wrenched away. I had just given birth in a most difficult way, I was at least fifty pounds overweight and suffering from the shock of having a second sick baby – one who was blessed with an even greater defect than his older brother.

I sat with Kyle every day, nursing him, holding him and worrying. One day I was holding Kyle in one arm and a cup of coffee in the other when a nurse told me that what I was doing was very dangerous. Since I thought I was being so careful, it never occurred to me that I could burn him. I placed my drink on a shelf over ten feet away and took a few sips only after returning Kyle to his crib.

Gradually Kyle was weaned from oxygen onto room air. After running more and more tests, they decided they no longer had any reason to keep him, although since it was Sunday, he couldn't be officially discharged. We would have to return in a day or two to take care of the paperwork, but in the interim we took him and ran. We were desperately nervous. I was afraid to dress him and take him out of the hospital. We drove to Wayne's parents' house because we didn't feel ready to be alone with him. After a joyous welcome, after undressing him and caring for him outside of a hospital setting, I began to feel more confident. We drove home to show Kyle his new bedroom.

The next day was full of excitement. Kyle's bellybutton fell off, which, of course, allowed for his first bath. It was nice to be able to do normal things with our infant that didn't entail medical procedure. Since I didn't quite know what to do with babies when I wasn't picking up lost bellybuttons and giving baths, I figured his baby swing would be a excellent option. I plopped that baby in the swing, wound it up and let it fly. He dutifully gazed around and eventually drifted off.

His first full day home was a great success. The following day brought an invitation from Wayne to go to the beauty parlour, since, as he so succinctly put it, I looked like I had "just come down off the side of a mountain." He offered to take me to the salon and bring Kyle to the hospital to be discharged. The nurses loved him and thought he was the most generous and thoughtful father. They fawned over him and Kyle and made him feel fantastic. I was meanwhile sitting in a chair, hunched over a colour chart composed of swatches of fake dyed hair.

"I want red, really red," I said.

The hairdresser should have considered my mental state and fluctuating hormones. She gave me red hair. And curls. Big ringlets à la Annie. When I stepped outside to wait for Wayne, he drove right by me. He denied it was on purpose, claiming that he didn't recognize me. He was being kind. I was very large, with a mass of red ringlets ablaze atop my head. In the bright sunshine, the sight of me must have blinded him.

Both grandmothers came to cook and clean and baby-sit. Winston took us all out for supper. The neighbours on the corner brought muffins. They said they could not stop thinking about Kyle and his heart problem. Kyle had his two-week checkup and had gained almost a pound and grown half an inch.

I was very depressed. I was very afraid. I was trying very hard not to feel that way, but I was so tired. Kyle was up almost all night, every night, and I was exhausted. By then, everyone had gone home and we were left all alone. I had to cope by myself. Wayne had to work and needed to sleep.

A few days later the power went out. When you use electric heat, a blackout can be a serious matter. The house began to get cold very quickly. I called Hydro Quebec and explained my predicament.

"I gave birth two weeks ago, my baby is very sick and needs to have open-heart surgery, and now the power has gone out." By this point I was already crying. "We need to have heat or we will freeze."

The woman on the other end of the line sounded as if she was going to cry too. "We'll have your power back on in an hour, I promise."

The lights flickered in less time than that and the baseboard heaters surged to life.

Early the next morning I suddenly had no strength in my arms. I lowered Kyle to the carpeted floor of his bedroom where I had been holding him in the rocking chair. He lay quietly, since he didn't have enough oxygen to cry. The doctor had warned me never to let him cry for more than five minutes. I watched him on the floor and wished that a giant bird would come, swoop down and carry him off in its beak. I was afraid to love him, because I was afraid he was going to die.

11
IT'S NEVER BEEN DONE

It was early April and the sun made an appearance. The always-wrong weatherman had called for more showers, but I was glad to see some brightness emerging from behind the omni-present clouds. Today was Kyle's first cardiac appointment at the Montreal Children's Hospital.

Dr. James E. Gibbons rose to meet us in his little office. He was semi-retired and had a good dose of white hair atop his kindly face. He held Kyle with an assurance that only decades of practice can bring. He listened to his heart, measured his height and weight, and after asking me a few questions, gave him a good once over. Then he sat me down, with Kyle still in his arms, and said, "His colour is good, his heart rate, eating habits, growth, weight are all great. We might even put off his first surgery until his first birthday."

Besides all the wonderful news I was hearing, I noticed how the doctor said it. All the little things that he wasn't saying were conveyed in his manner and transmitted to me. He was telling me that my son was healthy, except for his defective heart, that Kyle was going to live and we were all going to be fine. He gave me courage and made me feel like I could actually do this thing. I was grateful to him for giving me hope.

Our house on Roundtree had been taken off the market during all the upset that surrounded Kyle's birth. Three weeks after the delivery, on April 9, 1993, we received an acceptable offer and signed the papers. We bought the house on Dugas in Pierrefonds and were set to move at the end of June.

It was an extremely challenging time in our lives. Wayne was also waiting to hear about a job offer after an interview the previous week. Even with all the changes, we managed to live with some modicum of normalcy. My sister invited us over for pizza to celebrate the purchase of our new home. We arrived with Matthew and Kyle and a bottle of red wine. Paul was on the phone ordering an extra large all-dressed house special and Lorraine was laying out paper plates and napkins. She ran to hug me and took the baby out of my arms. She was pregnant and due in about six months, and was happy we were going to be neighbours.

Lorraine and Paul bought a house on the street three years previously, and we had first noticed the three-bedroom bungalow for sale by owner on another visit. I was happy but distracted by Kyle's health and told her all about my visit to Dr. Gibbons. I was relieved that someone was able to make me feel positive about my baby. All previous meetings with the other cardiologist had increased my certainty that he was doomed. Especially comments like, "He may need a heart transplant when he is an adult." Did I really need to hear stuff like that, something that may or may not happen twenty-five years down the road? We had a good time, though Lorraine and I didn't drink the wine. Lorraine commented that she couldn't wait to have her baby so that she could really party again. I felt I just couldn't indulge myself anymore. My life had taken a serious turn.

The next month passed fairly calmly. Kyle was growing and looked fine and I was beginning to relax enough to enjoy him. He began sleeping better and his decreasing nocturnal demands allowed me a little more rest.

Kyle was scheduled for a consultation with his surgeon in the last week of May. It was on a Friday, and he had already had a heart catheterization with Dr. Jutras on the previous Tuesday. He had stayed in the hospital for two days. We were going to hear the results.

We were ushered into Dr. Christo Tchervenkov's spacious office after the cardiology team had run another battery of tests. I asked him about a series of over twenty photographs of young patients with different doctors that hung on his wall. He explained that every year the resident pediatric cardiac surgeon was photographed with a special patient. "That's me in the second row," he said.

I liked this man very much. He was solid with dark hair and reminded me of Hercule Poirot of Agatha Christie fame, except without the penguin's waddle. Like the great detective, he was from Belgium and he loved living in Montreal. His wife, brother and both parents were doctors. He smiled at us, but it was a tired and sorry attempt. Dr. Jutras stood next to the famed surgeon. He looked much younger and slimmer as he towered over the seated specialist. Dr. Tchervenkov described Kyle's condition.

"Kyle has tricuspid atresia, a restrictive atrial septal defect, restrictive bulbar ventricular foramen, with severe cyanosis. His catheterization revealed that we are dealing with an obvious case of tricuspid atresia. The right pulmonary artery is 4.7 millimetres in diametre, the left pulmonary artery is 5.0 millimetres and the restrictive bulbar ventricular foramen has decreased in diametre from 6.0 to 3.0 millimetres. Kyle's oxygen saturation is in the mid-seventies. We are going to have to operate before June 1. That is not the issue here.

"What we must ask you is to choose between two options. We can do the traditional surgery, which is just a holding procedure to allow us to do a bi-directional Glenn anastomosis further down the road. Kyle would still need a third operation, the Fontan procedure, a couple of years later."

While he spoke, the doctor was gesticulating towards a colourful, larger-than-life model of a heart. It was mesmerizing to focus on what he was saying and trying to connect it all to my little baby.

"We are offering you an alternative," he continued. "Kyle could have the Glenn next week, completely avoiding the first open-heart surgery."

We were both stunned. I hadn't expected this kind of news. Kyle was healthy. The surgery wasn't going to be until his first birthday. It was so clinical, so technical and so very hard to comprehend.

"Are you sure you have to operate now?" Wayne asked.

"There is no question that we have to open up the hole in his heart so that he can live. The only question is, which operation do we perform now?" Dr. Tchervenkov sat forward on his leather, swivel chair. He was concerned and his anxiety made the decision seem even more grave.

"Why wouldn't we just skip the holding procedure and go right to the second operation?" I asked.

I looked at both doctors and then at Wayne. He had a pained expression and shrugged his shoulders helplessly.

"That's an excellent question. The Glenn shunt has only been attempted once before on a baby under six months, and unfortunately that baby didn't make it. But we have every reason to believe that Kyle will be fine. He is an excellent candidate. You can't even tell that Kyle is cardiac to look at him."

It was true. Every time we came to the hospital for an appointment, someone would invariably ask if he was indeed a cardiac patient, and comment that he didn't even look sick.

I was grasping about in my head for some tidbit of information that would help me decide on the correct course of action. I asked what were his chances.

Dr. Jutras explained that they couldn't answer that question. "As we said, the only other baby died. But we think Kyle has a really good chance. Ultimately this is a decision both of you have to make. And it's a decision you have to make today."

Wayne and I managed to stumble out of the surgeon's office. He held my hand and we wandered into a small family room. He shut the door. I sat on the couch and Wayne pulled up a folding chair to face me. He dropped his head into his upturned hands, and I put both arms around his shoulders.

"What are we going to do?" he asked.

I said that the Glenn was the only way. We had to save Kyle any pain that we could. One less surgery was the way to go.

I had my doubts, I certainly had my fears, but I had to hold myself together at this crucial juncture in our parenting life. It only made sense to follow the advice of the doctors. They were as sure as they could be that this was the best decision, the only sound choice. Now we had to trust in them and allow them to go ahead with the riskier operation. Our baby's life was at stake either way. It was time to put our faith somewhere and reach a conclusion. Even though Kyle stood a greater chance of dying, we couldn't pass up this opportunity to avert a surgical intervention. In the end, we had no real choice. The surgery would proceed the following Tuesday or Thursday.

We had a christening to organize. Wayne called his aunt Noella, who was working part time at a French Catholic church in Blainville, approximately forty minutes from our home. She managed to arrange a private ceremony for that Sunday after worship. Wayne and I asked our friends Steve and Kathy King to to be godfather and godmother. Kathy was a nurse and a mother and could, more than anyone, understand my pain. Steve was a single man with no children, but he was a long-time buddy to Wayne and cared about him a lot. They both agreed and along with Wayne's maternal aunts, our parents, assorted siblings and various close friends, we held a baptism.

The church had a modern facade, with a sloped roof and without a bell tower. Wide steps ran across the front of the building. Wayne and I huddled around the altar with Kathy and Steve, while Kyle lay in the middle. Two rows of pews were filled with guests in front of us. I was trying my damnedest not to cry, as it felt more like a funeral than a celebration of the birth of a child.

The ceremony was beautiful. The priest held Kyle up over his head and sang to him in a voice pure and clear. When he dabbed my son's head with holy water, I used the diversion of showing Kyle's incongruous red socks to prevent any crying. He was angelic in his long, white lace christening gown. He had a matching cap tied around his head and a bluish tinge around his mouth. He lay quietly as if observing everyone carefully. He was not allowed to cry at all and was on Propranaolol, a heart medication, that slowed down his heart muscle. His face was pinched and even I was seeing the effects of oxygen deprivation. His oxygen saturation level was going down daily, as the hole in his heart continued to shrink.

After the service, some of us went to a friend's parents' place in Rosemere for a small party. His mother got some KFC and everyone had chicken and either soft drinks or beer. Wayne carried a tightly bundled Kyle around in his arms and fashioned a daisy chain crown for his son's head. Kyle had been stripped of his baptismal gown and cap in a hurry by a father who thought his boy shouldn't be wearing a dress. It was a bittersweet afternoon and the sun shone as if blessing us all. Wayne and I leaned on each other for strength. By some unfathomable signal, I would alert him that I was about to fall apart and he would hold me or try to make me laugh. If I saw that he was failing, I would get close enough to try to pass him some of my strength for him to gather by osmosis.

Wayne was leaning against the wall outside the brick bungalow and I came to stand beside him. Kyle lay in his arms between us. We formed a protective shield around our baby. Wayne commented on how beautiful the service was. He seemed relieved that the baptism was over. I sensed that he was now focused on the upcoming surgery. It would have helped us to have an exact date to fixate on.

That Tuesday, we received a phone call that the surgery would be on Thursday and that we were expected to come to the hospital on Wednesday by 10 a.m.. My mother and I brought him in and we stayed for the day while Kyle underwent various pre-op tests and gave up vials of blood for blood work. Kyle was being his usual charming self and his cooing and killer smiles utterly charmed the blood technician. It was extremely difficult to leave him at the end of the day and only the knowledge that our sacrifice would help save his life made me walk out the door.

The morning of the surgery Wayne and I left the house with my mother at 5 a.m.. I was so intent on the day's proceedings that I completely missed if the sky was light or dark or if the weather was cloudy or clear. It was May 27 and the temperature was of no consequence. I was completely absorbed with what was about to take place. My mother was worried about us and really worried about Kyle. She said, "He's protected, he's under the protection of Holy Mary. He's going to be fine."

My mother was not a religious person by nature. We never attended church as children except for the occasional Christmas service. This spiritual bent to her prognosticating was most unusual.

There was little traffic on the road and we made good time to the hospital. We were scheduled for the first of two open-heart surgeries that day. Our placement had been switched several times in the previous two days, until it was finally settled. I was glad that we were going first. It was hard enough waiting until 9 a.m. for the surgery. Sitting around all day with a hungry infant would have been virtually impossible.

The nurses stopped giving Kyle fluids by mouth at midnight, and when I went in to see Kyle, I was expecting him to be hungry. My breasts were exploding with milk, but my baby just lay there. So strangely quiet, overcome by some sort of pre-operative inertia.

At 7 a.m. we all went up to surgery to wait in a large room filled with all sorts of toys. There was another family there ahead of us. A mother, a father and a young girl were waiting in the corner and the woman was crying. I carried my silent bundle over to the family and asked what was the matter.

The mother pulled the girl closer and pointed at her ear. "They're going to operate. They're going to remove *that*," she said, whereupon she continued to weep.

The child had a small growth below her right ear. It would probably take all of ten minutes with a local anesthetic. As the family had no curiosity about us, I wandered back over to Wayne and my mother.

The time passed very slowly and the hour for them to take Kyle away came and went. We waited another half-hour before a nurse came out and told us that the heart-lung machine operator had been delayed in traffic and had only just arrived. With all the switching of start times, he had been misinformed about when he was due at the hospital and had only been notified that morning. We waited some more, while Kyle's condition deteriorated further. The nurses on both floors had delegated the monitoring of his vitals to the other. In the interim he was being followed by neither. He became increasingly blue-tinged and lethargic. He was not responsive to any stimulus and seemed barely conscious. Finally the team opened the wide sliding doors and stood before us.

We had previously met the anesthetist, who explained how they were going to induce moderate hypothermia down to 28° C and operate in cardiopulmonary bypass for approximately ninety minutes. "Kyle's saturation was down to the sixties yesterday," he said. "We're going to take good care of him today and fix him up."

There was no fixing what Kyle had, or rather, what he didn't have. A missing ventricle cannot be replaced. But the surgery was meant to move half of his body's blood flow so that he had better oxygenation. I didn't really understand everything that was going on, but I knew that they were going to cut into my tiny baby's sternum and heart and that he might not make it. I was praying furiously that he did.

Wayne was holding a stuffed Tigger and asked if he could put it on Kyle's gurney. A nurse with a colourful cloth cap and paper-wrapped shoes said he could. I lay Kyle down and they bore him off before I could change my mind.

My mother dragged us back down to Kyle's empty bed. The window was open and a subtle breeze played on my skin. Fragrance from flowering trees in the park across the road managed to find its way up my nose and reach my sensory receptors. I took a deep breath. It felt like I had forgotten to breathe for the past few hours.

The hours crawled by. At 12:15 p.m. a nurse notified us that Kyle had been "discontinued off cardiopulmonary bypass without any difficulty, maintaining oxygen saturation in the high eighties." At 3 o'clock the same nurse came to say we could see him.

Wayne and I stepped hesitantly into the ICU. Kyle lay on the first bed closest to the door. The tiny inflated form on the bed was hardly recognizable as our child. If it weren't for the stuffed Tigger on the bed above his head I could happily have imagined him as someone else's problem and gone in search of my own baby. He lay prone and naked. He looked terrible. He was swollen with two pounds of fluid and hooked up to a respirator with many monitors humming overhead. He had four pacemaker wires coming out of his body where his heart was supposed to be (two ventricular and two atrial), a chest drain and a catheter. A Glenn line was in his neck for food and medicine. I gasped and stood motionless. Wayne managed a sharp intake of breath and approached the side of the bed. When he gently touched Kyle's cheek, Kyle didn't move. He was unconscious.

A nurse glided over to stand between us. "He's doing well," she said. "He'll be in a drug induced comma for about three days. It will help him to heal." She attended to Kyle and began making notes about his condition. He was her only patient.

Dr. Jutras and Dr. Tchervenkov came over to see us. I fairly leapt to hug him and express my thanks. Wayne was overcome with gratitude and relief as well. He shook both of their hands.

Dr. Tchervenkov described Kyle's condition.

"His oxygen saturation dropped down into the twenties on the table and he was cyanotic, but I quickly placed a right-angled cannula in the inferior vena cava at the atrial caval junction and another high in the superior vena cava, and cardiopulmonary bypass was begun. We will only know in seventy-two hours if we were successful. Kyle tolerated the procedure well and he is in stable condition. Try not to worry, he's receiving some of the best care in the world."

The good doctors moved on to the next patient and Wayne and I sat down to wait. Even though the surgeon spoke in a very clinical manner, he had informed us of where we stood and what to expect over the next little while. He also reminded me of how incredibly lucky we were to have the quality of care we did in Montreal.

Three days passed and I began to learn the meaning of the word patience. Every time something was removed, it was cause for celebration. Three days post-op and they stopped his antibiotics. Four days and they removed his Glenn line and stopped the heart medication Amniron. Kyle opened his eyes between the two events and looked at me as if I was a stranger. His delight at the sight and smell of me had disappeared into a cloudy haze of non-recognition.

We were told that he was going to live. Our nurse, Julie, stood over me after I had received the wonderful news. She told us that Dr. Jutras intended to stop the IV soon and that Kyle could then start on distilled sterile water and eventually breast milk. I was glad, because I had twenty bottles of breast milk stored at the hospital. Kyle was doing well. He was recovering quickly but not quickly enough.

After eight days I was so exhausted that I began crying constantly. Kyle was fine. I was the one who needed to be admitted. I was wiped out and it was fortunate that Kyle was improving steadily, because I was losing my ability to cope. All his wires and drains had been removed and we had been sent back down to 7C. His vital signs were great, but I had observed some disturbing behavior. Kyle didn't seem to hold his head up in the same way – it tilted and listed to one side. He was very crabby, wasn't eating well and had a fierce diaper rash. He would barely make eye contact with me and had stopped smiling.

I loved him so much and it felt as if my heart was breaking at all the changes in him. I still attempted to breastfeed, but with my low energy level and his apparent unwillingness to suckle, the bottle was proving the easier route. He was wonderful, but I was so psychologically drained from the traumatic events and drama since his birth that I just couldn't do it any more. He started pushing his head back when I held him in my arms and he twisted his mouth around in a strange, completely unfunny manner.

He was discharged after a difficult two weeks. I gave up breast-feeding. My milk production had reduced to a trickle and Kyle was not hungry enough to increase the amount of milk I was producing. I was devastated at having to wean him so early. Wayne brought home bottles and formula. We had to move into the new house in a few days and I began packing.

Regina helped me care for Kyle and prepare for the move. She was a bundle of energy and packed just about every box. I fed Kyle and watched him sleep and within a few days I had recovered a modicum of energy.

Kyle stayed at my sister's with my mother in attendance. With a bunch of Wayne's male friends and lots of beer and pizza, Wayne and I finally moved into our first new home.

Until Kyle's room was ready, his crib was placed in the livingroom. He was sleeping through the night and after a few days I decided to stay up late to watch a movie. I was really enjoying the picture and felt like a normal person, staying up past my bedtime and watching television. Then Kyle decided he wasn't quite cured of his nocturnal habit. He began crying at 2 a.m. and had loose stool. He also had a bad cough and was sneezing.

I took him to see Dr. Young, his pediatrician, who reassured me that it was just his teeth coming in. I wanted to be sure that he was okay, I wanted everything to be over and for him to be like other babies.

He wasn't and he never would be, but his next cardiology clinic visit was uplifting.

"He's continuing with his excellent progress," said Dr. Gibbons. "Kyle is vigorous, alert, playful and asymptomatic. His oximetre saturation is eighty-eight percent and his weight is in the fiftieth percentile. His palpation was good and I think the Fontan can wait for a few years."

I was ecstatic. The doctors didn't want to see Kyle until June of the next year.

I rushed home to tell Wayne. I prepared a special dinner of manicotti and salad. Wayne came in clutching a dozen red roses, a box containing a suede vest and a black felt hat of the type worn in Argentina, on horseback. This was definitely not in our budget. I poured two glasses of a decent red wine and told Wayne what the doctor had said about Kyle. Wayne smiled and asked if I'd like to get married.

I was stunned and stood gaping at him like a hooked and landed speckled trout.

"What are you talking about?"

"Well, I've already proposed. Now all we have to do is get the rings."

If I could have leapt over the table and landed in his lap without overturning the pasta, I would have. He came around the table and pulled me into his arms for a kiss. He said he'd seen a ring he liked on a guy at the garage. Since when was Wayne checking out the rings on other guys?

"It's called a Claddah ring," Wayne continued. "It has a heart for love, two hands for friendship and a crown for loyalty. It's Irish." I'd seen the same ring on a woman at Kathy's cottage about six years earlier and thought it was the most beautiful ring I had ever seen. Apparently, so did Wayne.

Wayne took me out for dinner about a month later. We went to an upscale Chinese restaurant, and sometime between dinner and the green tea, he went down on one knee and proposed.

"Will you do me the honour of being my wife?"

It was simple, direct and expected. I told him he could get up off his knee. He opened up the jewelry boxes he had pulled from inside his lapel pocket. One brown velvet box held a man's wedding band with the heart and cuffs in rodian and the crown and hands in gold. My wedding ring was similar, but infinitely more feminine, with an engagement ring that fit intricately together with the band. It had a lovely diamond, which proved to me that Wayne really meant it this time. I could plan the wedding.

Not long before this surprising turn of events, Myrna told me about a friend, Eliza, who had eloped to Plattsburg, New York, and worn a gold lace suit to her wedding. She drove me over to Eliza's townhouse, and after she had shown me the suit, I asked if I could borrow it.

Eliza told me all about her elopement. She and her husband had driven down to the courthouse in Old Plattsburg. She even gave me the name and number of the judge who married them. "You don't need blood tests or anything," she added. "The best part is, it only costs twenty-five bucks."

I went home and hid my outfit in the closet. I told Wayne I had picked up my dress but that it was really rather plain. I explained what Eliza had said about her elopement. Wayne got on the phone to ask Kerry to be his best man. Kerry's girlfriend Kate offered to be my maid of honour.

"Do people bring witnesses when they're running off to get married?" I wondered aloud.

"Why not?" said Wayne.

We decided to do it over Thanksgiving weekend. We even invited our parents, except Wayne's said they would rather keep Kyle while we were getting hitched.

Wayne was sure moving things along. I knew that he was only getting married to make me happy and because we had had a child together. Now that Kyle was out of immediate danger, Wayne was doing what he could to please me. He had told me many times that he couldn't be more committed and that he wasn't going anywhere.

Wayne's parents agreed to bring Kyle up north with them. They even offered to host a small reception on the evening of our return. My parents would meet us in Plattsburg on Saturday morning with Kerry and Kate. An unexpected bonus was that Kate was a professional wedding photographer. She would make us an album as a wedding present.

Since Monday was a holiday for Thanksgiving, we decided to take the weekend off. Wayne had recently started a new job and my maternity leave was over and I was back at the dentist's office. I called the judge and arranged for him to meet us at noon on October 9. We planned to drive down to New York on the Friday before. Kyle, who was now seven months old, was finally going to have married parents.

Wayne packed a suit, but needed a white shirt and possibly a bow tie. I had stashed my gold suit and a pair of glittery gold Givenchy stockings, but lacked a pair of shoes. We drove to the courthouse and registered the marriage within the twenty-four hour limit. We had to prove that we were both not married to anyone else and that we lived where we said we did.

We went shopping at a small wedding boutique and found a used, ruffled, but not too frilly tuxedo shirt, a blue, yellow and green bow tie and a matching cummerbund for Wayne. At a Payless, I found the perfect pair of gold pumps for only five dollars, after the sales clerk had sworn they only carried bronze shoes. I was very excited about the evening to come.

At dinner, Wayne ordered champagne and strawberries and chocolate. Over tall flutes of very fine French bubbly, he fed me strawberries and toasted me. "Your eyes are so beautiful, I know where Kyle gets his from. You are my dream girl you know. I can't wait to marry you."

I couldn't believe it was finally happening. I was so happy. Wayne continued to gaze into my eyes in the most romantic manner possible until all I could think about was getting him back to our room. This particular evening has remained one of my fondest memories of our journey together.

The following morning I awoke in a golden flush of joy. How different this day was from my previous wedding twelve years before. I had no jitters, no second thoughts and was filled with a sense of certainty and calm. Even though I was still overweight from having just had a baby, I barely thought about it. Wayne accepted me completely and allowed me to feel comfortable about myself.

I showered and began to style my hair. My parents arrived just ahead of Kerry and Kate. Kate brought me dried flowers for my bouquet and was wearing my divorce dress of polka-dotted, cream silk. With a messy mop of blond curls, she looked ravishing. My father brought out the video camera and began to film me doing my hair, with my mother admonishing him to stop.

After showering and changing into a suit and tie, Wayne and Kerry left to fortify themselves with a pre-wedding drink.

"You better be there at noon sharp," I whispered into his departing ear.

"Don't you worry, I'll be there," he said over his shoulder, just as the door closed behind him.

Kate lounged on the bed. My parents sat in their formal attire on two stiff hotel chairs. I was applying makeup as carefully as an undertaker would on his former boss. I put on the skirt of gold lace with the elasticized waist and managed to close the hooks and eyes of the jacket. My high heels were exactly that, and I tottered out to my father's waiting car. Kate and my mother had me pose getting in and waving like the queen of England sitting in the back seat. We drove to the old courthouse. We parked about a hundred feet away and watched Wayne and Kerry standing by the entrance.

The boys were pacing slightly and waved over to us in the car. I didn't want Wayne to see me before the ceremony, so we held our positions until the judge arrived. By 12:15, I was beginning to get nervous. At 12:30, Wayne went to the pay phone on the corner and called the police to find out the judge's phone number. After conferencing with my father, it was agreed that my dad and I would drive over to the judge's house to find out what the delay was. My father, with his twisted sense of humour, filmed the entire episode.

The minute I exited the car, the judge's wife came bounding out the front door. This was quite a feat, considering she was well over sixty and a tad shy of five feet tall. She testily responded to my inquiries about her husband, claiming the appointment had been made for 1 p.m.. No entreaties on my part could convince her otherwise, and we were sent back to the courthouse to await his lordship.

He did indeed show up a few minutes later and, after entering the courthouse with Wayne and Kerry, summoned the bridal party at 1 p.m. on the nose. My mother went in first to videotape the procession and my dad walked me down the aisle. Wayne's face when he saw my outfit was worth the wait. He was fairly popping out of his skin with happiness and seemed eager to proceed with the ceremony. With only a few nervous pauses over some of the words, a mild fumble with the ring and checking out our witnesses when the judge asked if there were objections, our wedding went into the history books. There was some good-natured jostling and ribbing as we posed and signed the registrar.

My father asked if there was a good restaurant nearby where we could get something to eat. The judge directed us to a Chinese restaurant down the road and decided to join us when we extended the invitation. We ended up having a great meal, with the waitress serenading us with "The Rose" by Bette Midler.

Afterwards, Kate insisted on taking more pictures, even though the sky threatened rain at any moment. We pulled up to the edge of a cornfield and my mother and Kate took a few shots. The setting turned out to be magnificent: golden stripped stalks of corn towering over us, with an almost black mid-afternoon sky providing our backdrop.

My parents left for home and we drove to the Black Lantern Inn in Vermont, followed by Kerry and Kate. The rain thundered down for the entire drive and I itched and twisted in my seat in the humidity and my fancy suit. Kate and Kerry beat us to the inn and insisted we take more pictures the minute we had arrived. We posed for another hour while my makeup finished its meltdown and my hair decided it had had enough and went its own way. Kerry bought us a bottle of champagne and we got silly. As patrons entered the bar of the inn, Wayne would shout out that we had just gotten married. This would invariably cause them to buy us a drink and join the party.

We finally turned in after midnight. Our room was just larger than the bed. To change out of our wedding attire, we had to take turns undressing while the other person waited in the hallway. I donned a new nightgown. This time, it was appreciated. I crawled over Wayne to get to my side of the bed next to the window. I climbed under the covers next to my new husband and lay back exhausted on the pillow. He pulled back the blankets and gazed at me for a long moment and then announced, with touching sincerity, "You are almost too beautiful, I can't believe it." There has never been a new bride that was loved so well.

The following day, the four of us took the gondola to the top of Jay peak. Down in the valley below we spotted cows and verdant green grass. Up on the mountaintop we experienced a blizzard. We stood in the foot-deep snow and felt, briefly, the wind whipping the air around us in mini-cyclones. The men stood resolute with upturned collars and shivered in the unexpected cold. We hurried back into the gondola for the passage down and an escape from winter.

Kerry and Kate left after lunch. Wayne and I were finally alone. We dined at the Black Lantern Inn and the next day drove to Stowe, Vermont to walk around. Our return home was a celebratory drive that culminated with a reception of about thirty people at the Rooney's home. Kate and Kerry were there also, and Kate took the last of the pictures for our wedding album. We received many gifts and were toasted many, many more times. Kyle slept through most of the evening in just about everybody's arms. He was passed around the room in the loving embraces of family and friends. I felt content and that I had done the right thing with the right person.

During the drive home, Wayne had commented that we should elope more often. I definitely agreed, but only about the going away part. I wasn't getting married ever again.

The next month I watched Kyle backstroke his way across the floor, to his own delight and the delight of all onlookers. He was so proud of his accomplishment, which explained why he was crammed in the corner of his crib in the mornings. He flipped and flopped all over my bed when I put him down to play and could snatch Wayne's glasses off his face faster than Wayne could keep them on. With Kyle's newfound prowess, I was reminded of the passage of time. I remembered to stop and enjoy my son.

It was at the end of another frenetic day and we had just finished up the evening bath. There he was, looking all fat and wet. Joy was flowing from his Buddha body and it felt wonderful to bask in his sunshine. I told him, "I love you my lovely."

12
SECOND OPEN
HEART SURGERY

Kyle's first Christmas was an extraordinary occasion. Kyle was alive and though I was very much afraid that he could still die during the next surgery, I was determined to be grateful for his presence every day. Both families came for the celebration, mine on Christmas Eve and Wayne's the following day. On December 24, my mother and father, my sister and Paul and their new baby, and my brother Anthony and his new baby, all converged on our new home to welcome the holidays. Kyle was crawling on his knees, but it was a strange one-legged maneuver, with a pull and a drag to boot. He tried out a new laugh and had everyone amused. He received a padded riding pony and Matthew got a Sega game system. Matthew told me he loved Kyle more than his Sega. "Just kidding!" he said. "I love him much more than my Sega."

I had kept a journal since I had learned that I was pregnant with Matthew, and upon comparison of my previous entries to a recent notation, I perceived a more spiritual trend. I wrote, "All I ever ask from Life, first and foremost, is that Kyle have a healthy life. Please let him live." I was searching for something and early the next year, I found it.

I was introduced to Al-Anon, a twelve-step group, by an acquaintance named Susan. It was formed as non-alcoholic members of A.A. began meeting separately to help friends and families of alcoholics. I had told her I was feeling lost and she immediately asked if I had any alcoholics in my life. I said no, but upon reflection I mentioned that my mother had been raised in an alcoholic home with a grandmother who had ensured chaos.

An Al-Anon meeting is not unlike a one-armed nun walking into a room full of other one-armed nuns. Everyone welcomed me without question. I was never asked to speak or for money and something was abundantly clear from the first – what was said there, stayed there. We sat around the room of the church in chairs in varying states of decay. There were women and some men, from young to old. They said their names and each spoke in turn about the topic of the evening. That week's chair had chosen the subject of fear and read two selections from Al-Anon literature and then she opened the floor. I said my name and began to listen. Rather than sharing about the alcoholic in their lives, they talked about fear and how it touched their own lives, and how they were using the tools of Al-Anon to replace fear with faith.

It may have been a musty, old vestibule in which we sat, but the warmth and love that I felt from all present made me relax and appreciate that I was not alone. I attended many meetings in the two years before Kyle's next operation and I gained invaluable tools with which to deal with life. I learned acceptance, and not to accept unacceptable behavior. The first step of the twelve step program taught me that I was powerless over everything except myself. The slogans helped me to cope with everyday situations: "Live and Let Live," "One Day at a Time" and "Let Go and Let God" became staples of my life. The serenity prayer became a mantra for times when things got just too difficult:

God, grant me the serenity
to accept the things I cannot change,
the courage to change the things I can,
and the wisdom to know the difference.

The program was not religious, but it was spiritual and I became familiar with the idea of having a higher power in my life, one that I chose to call God. For some people that concept could have been a tree or even a rock. The idea that there was something bigger, something more powerful than myself that I could turn to at anytime, was truly a gift. Every morning I asked for guidance and every night before I went to sleep, I said a prayer of gratitude for my day. No matter how extremely bad it seemed at the time, I said thank you. I gave thanks for all the wonderful things in my world and tried to see only the good. I attended conferences and many intensive weekends. I made many friends in the program, friends that were there for me anytime that I needed them and still are to this day.

Kyle turned one on March 14 and both families and many friends came over for chocolate cake. I wanted a cheesecake but Wayne overruled me and called my girlfriend Diane to change the order. He asked for an Ernie cake instead. Wayne wanted to ensure that his son had his favourite character from Sesame Street on his first birthday cake. Just that day, when Wayne and Kyle were watching Sesame Street, Kyle spotted Ernie, crawled to his room and came back with his Ernie puppet. He held him up to the television and gave him a kiss.

They all came, with presents, with balloons and with big smiles. Upon seeing Kyle's clean face, Wayne's aunt Simone said, "We have to have some cake on him for the pictures." She proceeded to rub a dab of cake on his nose and a smidgen at the corners of his mouth.

Kyle was very excited. Just as the festivities began he pulled his high chair down on top of himself in an aborted attempt at climbing up into it. He suffered a black eye, which also added to the birthday pictures. Matthew was very attentive to Kyle, and as I brought out the cake, he huddled close and whispered "happy birthday" in his ear.

Long after the balloons had withered and expired, Kyle pointed up to where they had been.

"They went bye-bye," I said.

He waved and waved again. He hadn't started to walk yet but he could say, "Oh gee," and, "Daddy." Wayne was in tears the first time he heard him speak.

The next year passed quickly and relatively uneventfully. Matthew adjusted to everything and Kyle grew and learned to talk in sentences. He could sing songs and count to fifteen. He was also very polite and could say "please," "thank you" and "you're welcome." He had very positive checkups and was due for a heart catheterization at the end of the month. We thought constantly about his next surgery.

One night, Wayne and I were sitting at the kitchen table planning Kyle's second birthday party. The children were asleep and the lights were dimmed. We had had another Quebec snow storm and the last of the flakes were falling softly. Our hands were wrapped around steaming mugs of mint tea, and as we were discussing who to invite, I blurted out that I couldn't believe Kyle was two.

"I never thought we'd get this far. It was virtually an impossible reality for me." I slumped in my chair and looked at Wayne. He turned his sad blue eyes on me.

"We still have to get through his last surgery. Let's just enjoy him for today."

That summer the weather was spectacular. I didn't take a vacation because I wanted to take it all at once when Kyle was in the hospital. At Halloween, he dressed up as a pirate. We hadn't made it fifty feet before he turned to me, arms strained heavenward, and asked to be picked up since he was tired. In the fading light, I could see that familiar tinge of blue around his mouth and felt fear grip my heart. The trees were shedding the last of their foliage and the wind was rising. My two sons and I trudged several more blocks with Kyle wrapped in my arms and Matthew, in a Batman costume, bringing up the rear.

We had a quiet family Christmas and during the week between Christmas and New Year's, I took him for a routine checkup. The doctor came back to me after all the tests and set the operation date for January 25. The second before he gave the date, I had the overwhelming impression that he would say January 23. I asked if he really meant the twenty-third.

"No," he responded, "I said the twenty-fifth. We'll see you both then." He tapped Kyle's nose and gave me a mustachioed grin. His bedside manner had warmed up significantly since our first meeting after Kyle's birth and his clinical rendition of my baby's defective heart, but it still seemed such an effort.

Kyle's surgery was only three weeks and five days off. When I reached home I began calling both sets of parents and our three sisters. They all said they would start praying, except for Winston, who was probably praying but wouldn't talk about it. Matthew was with my parents and was leaving for Mexico with his dad the next week. He would be back before the surgery.

On Friday, January 19, we were summoned to the surgeon's office once again. We entered older, wiser and infinitely more experienced than our first visit. We sat poised opposite Dr. Tchervenkov in two deep mahogany leather chairs. The weak winter sun strained to penetrate the glass of his arched windows. His office door was closed to the hospital sounds and smells. I looked at the wall of fame and was pleased to see Kyle and Dr. Daniel Marelli represented as the doctor and patient for 1993.

Kyle was perched on the smiling doctor's left thigh and cradled in the crook of his arm. A large hand with long, solid fingers held him securely across the front of his sailor's suit. Kyle's pudgy cheeks almost rolled down to his neck and he appeared absorbed by the camera. Our surgeon looked at us with those same tired eyes and explained Kyle's prognosis.

"Since Kyle was able to skip the initial stage, which would have been a systemic pulmonary shunt, he underwent a primary Glenn shunt at ten weeks of age. He will be readmitted for the completion of the Fontan operation, which will be performed by direct atrial pulmonary anastomosis between the atrial appendage and the divided main pulmonary artery. You could be cancelled at any time because ICU is overcrowded."

He explained the procedure and after we had exhausted our store of questions and thanked him, we went home.

On Saturday afternoon, Wendy and Pierre came over with lasagna and brownies. Wendy fussed over Kyle, who patiently stood for her caresses and hair mussing. She pinned him on the couch after dinner and asked him to get a book so she could read him a story. Kyle went to his room to get *The Three Little Pigs*, walking because he couldn't run and had never run in his life. They snuggled on the sofa and Wayne and I sat in the love seat holding hands. It was once again snowing but I welcomed the inevitable elements and my thoughts turned to Kyle and to God.

I said to Him, "He's yours. I turn him completely over to you, to do what you will. If you decide to take him, I'll have to understand, and if you don't, I'll be eternally grateful. I won't beg you to save him. Thy will be done."

I felt at peace and comforted. Wayne's grip on my hand tightened as if he sensed what I had just experienced. He leaned into me and tipped his head onto my shoulder.

"I love him so much."

"I know," I whispered. "I do too."

Sunday brought Winston and Regina and her famous shepherd's pie. This was a concoction of corn, ground beef and mashed potato topping that French Canadians call "pâté chinois," Chinese pie, for reasons unknown. Kyle ate like it was his last meal and we allowed him three deserts. The hospital food he was about to face was barely edible and it would be weeks before he could have another home cooked meal. Regina was happy to stuff her only grandson full of her cooking and encouraged him to eat heartily. They slept over and left early in the morning.

Monday was my last scheduled workday and was the longest of my life. I wore a forest green suede suit with a full skirt, long sleeves and a cowl neck. It was very expensive and had been given to me by Jackie, my former mother-in-law, who had remained part of my life. She had met Wayne several times and thought he was extremely handsome. "Those blue eyes," she would say. "He's definitely a keeper."

For a better part of the morning I struggled to concentrate on my work, anything to take my mind off what lay ahead. My co-worker, Lainey, had been badgering me since I walked in. Her most recent sally left me unhinged.

"How is it," she asked, "that you're going to be gone for five weeks? There's a lot of work to be done." She was five-foot-five of vindictive vitriol. She had rivulets of auburn hair that ran down her lithe back. She was smart, artistic and unsuited to office work. She was also my boss's cousin.

After her last barrage I barricaded myself in my boss's office. He came in and knelt beside my crumpled form in the corner, next to a box full of toothbrushes. He gently lifted me up and put me in his chair. I was crying and babbling about Lainey and had perspired so much that the suit was damp from my waist to my elbows. He drove me home at the end of the day, after letting me rest in his office undisturbed for the entire afternoon.

After fetching Kyle, I picked up Matthew at school and we walked in the front door at exactly 6:45 p.m.. The phone's shrill ring pierced the silence. After fumbling for the light, I grabbed the telephone's receiver and answered.

A female voice informed me that we needed to bring Kyle in right away to the Montreal Children's Hospital. His surgery had been bumped forward because a child with the same blood type was sick and his surgery had to be postponed.

I hung up in shock and told Matthew the news. He let out a ferocious wail and shrieked, "My brother's going to die." He was inconsolable and scaring Kyle, who looked at me with frightened eyes and a quivering bottom lip and chin. He couldn't articulate what he must have been feeling, but went over to his crying brother, put his arms around him and told him not to cry. He held his pale face next to Matthew's deep, Mexico-tanned skin, and turned to give him a kiss. The eldest of my two sons managed a weak smile.

Shortly thereafter, Mike picked up Matthew, once again providing support and understanding as he always did in a crisis. He stood in my door, clasping Matthew's hand tightly in his and said, "I'll take care of our son and you take care of Kyle. I know you can do it." He bent down and gave me a gentle kiss that brought a comforted smile to Matthew's worried face.

We were at the hospital in under an hour. It took quite a while to be admitted because they weren't expecting us until Wednesday, but Kyle eventually had a bed and we settled him down after some blood work and X-rays. Kyle was a real hit up in ICU for his weigh-in.

We were surprised to learn that the parents of the child that had developed a high fever were actually friends of Wayne. Though they had not spoken for over two years, Wayne had coincidentally called them that very morning about printing, as they were in the same business. Wayne now worked for himself and had a small office in our basement. They were inconsolable about the surgery being moved to some future date and we tried to make them feel a little better. After a bath, Kyle finally fell asleep, surrounded by his stuffed animals.

We went to the family room to sleep in pull-out chairs. The room was bland, with beige walls and large sealed windows. Drab curtains hung limply, blocking out the city's light pollution. I walked towards the sheet of glass and peered through an opening between the curtains down to the roof of the attached building. Steam poured skyward into the frigid air from tall funneled brick chimneys.

"I'm scared," I admitted. Wayne came over and stood behind me and held me in his arms.

"I know," he said, "but he's a tough little guy."

His warmth and strength seeped into my spirit and I felt transformed. Whatever the result tomorrow, we would handle it. Wayne managed to convert two chairs into beds and I changed into a nightgown. He settled down in his jeans and long-sleeved T-shirt. It was after 1:30 a.m. before I fell asleep.

The morning came swiftly and with a vengeance. It was not yet 5:00 a.m. and dawn's first light was still a couple of hours away. The nurse woke Wayne up, who attempted to rouse me. I was not a morning person and was confused. Brushing my teeth and changing into my clothes helped, but until I had a cup of coffee my brain was refusing to go into drive.

We got two cups from the coffee machine by the elevators. It was in a large area with two bathrooms and a public telephone. We sat in metal chairs with a thin layer of padded vinyl and sipped out of styrofoam cups. We didn't speak and the silence comforted me. I listened to the hum of the heating and ventilation system. The building was like a living entity with its rhythmic breathing and continuous pulse. Wayne drained his cup and tossed the remains into the garbage bin under the phone.

I followed his lead through the swinging doors back to 7C and our dozing child. A nurse was ahead of us and we followed her to Kyle's crib. He lay in angelic repose. His slumber was deep and peaceful. His lips were parted slightly and his breathing was regular. As she began to take his temperature, he woke up.

The next hour passed quickly. Kyle was so absorbed playing with puzzles that he never noticed he wasn't having breakfast. He was so quick, so smart, that I was scared about what another surgery, another hour-and-a-half bypass, another round of chilling his little body and stopping his heart, would do to his brain.

We trooped up to 10D. Kyle was in a gurney guided by a fabulous bald fellow named Peter, who sang the Spiderman song with Kyle ten times over. Kyle, who was also shaved, had chosen Tigger to accompany him into surgery, but even his plush friend was forgotten during the ride up. We waited anxiously while Kyle played with toys he had been too young to investigate on his first visit two-and-a-half years before. The doors slid open and a doctor appeared with a surgical nurse. The surgical resident, Dr. Renzo Tchicery, bent forward over Kyle and asked if he was ready to go. Kyle retrieved his stuffed animal and, clutching it to his chest, toddled over to Wayne and gave his father a big kiss. He planted another one on my cheek and declared happily that he was going to get a new heart. The nurse took his hand and he walked through the sliding doors away from us, possibly forever.

We sat transfixed for a long while. I willed the doors to reopen so I could retrieve my baby, but they never did.

Wayne left to meet our parents, who would be arriving soon. He disappeared into the elevator for the complicated journey from 10D to 7C, which involved changing elevators, several detours and a map to complete. I meandered past several closed doors until I came upon an opened, inviting office with a woman working at a typewriter. I felt drawn to her and entered the tiny cubicle and stood next to her desk. She looked up at me with kind eyes set in a broad Slavic face. She seemed almost to be expecting me.

"Is your child in surgery?" she asked, a wisp of auburn hair twisting out of the ponytail tied behind her head.

I explained with downcast eyes Kyle's operation and was stunned when she said that her son had had the same operation.

"He's fourteen now and plays soccer. Here's his picture." She proudly produced a photograph of a healthy looking young man with one foot balanced on a soccer ball. "They did it here when he was four and now look at him."

I was nodding madly and tears began to cascade freely down my face. This surgery was so huge and was performed only about a half dozen times a year. The coincidence of stumbling across another mother who had undergone the same thing seemed immense. She understood my weeping and gave me a hug. She said she'd come to see me in ICU in a couple of days. Fortified by my unexpected good fortune in finding her, I mumbled a brief thank you and found my way back to Wayne.

The grandmothers and one grandfather had joined him. They were headed to a waiting area on the second floor, which was equipped with a phone so we could receive information as the morning progressed. Winston was unable physically and emotionally to enter the hospital. We settled into our chairs and waited for the phone to ring.

Barry and Linda, friends from Al-Anon, came to complete the roster. Linda was petite and blond, with a small face and laughing green eyes. She had three children and eleven grandchildren. She hated going to hospitals, and her knees were knocking in her full-figured jeans. Her husband was long and lanky and balding. Wisps of grey hair thinly covered the back and sides of his handsome, well-shaped head. He was smart, funny and had a permanent twinkle in his eyes, because he knew that everything was going to work out. He and Linda had faith and they brought it with them to the hospital to share with us. Barry also brought a cribbage board and the men began a five-hour long tournament.

The women sat in a small circle, knees nearly touching and I was regaled with stories that were intended to keep my mind off my child's predicament. My mother nervously squeezed my hand and said, "I'm sure everything's going as well as can be expected. Kyle's protected and he's not going to die."

I wasn't sure whether or not he would live but I knew that it was out of my hands. Wayne twitched his head around and gave me a soul-searching gaze. He mouthed the words "I love you" and went back to pegging his hand. He appeared to be winning and with Barry that always meant a couple of bucks. My father fancied himself a good cribbage player and looked ruefully at the pegs that showed him to be in last place.

The phone rang and we collectively jumped in our seats. Wayne scrambled to grab the receiver and knocked it out of its cradle. He pulled it by its curly line and thrust it against his ear. He was brought up to date on Kyle's condition.

"Your son is out of cardiopulmonary bypass. He was in for ninety-eight minutes and it was discontinued without any difficulty, while maintaining excellent hemodynamics. The aortic cross-clamp time was fory-four minutes and his lowest temperature was 26.3° C. He's in good shape and will be in surgery for at least another hour or two."

Wayne hung up and hugged Barry, then my father and then worked his way to me. He kissed the top of my head tenderly and said, "Our baby's gonna make it." I didn't dissuade him and stoically returned to my chair. It ain't over until the fat lady sings.

Dr. Tchervenkov found our motley crew half-dozing, half-frantically pacing after the surgery. He stood before me, beaming.

"Kyle tolerated the procedure well and was transferred to 9D in stable condition. We have to be cautious for the next seventy-two hours, but all should go well."

I gave him a big, fat hug, which most likely embarrassed him. He stood stiffly while receiving my exuberant appreciation and seemed relieved when I finally released him. I was overjoyed and itching to see Kyle. We were like thoroughbreds at the Kentucky Derby when we were finally allowed out of the gate and to go up to ICU. We entered like two children finally allowed in to see the presents under the tree on Christmas morning. I was flabbergasted at the sight of my child, flabbergasted at the utter pinkness of him. He looked fantastic.

Our son was unconscious. My eyes hopped from his feet, to his ears, to his penis, to his fingers and back to his face. I never fully appreciated how blue he had been until I saw how pink he had become. He was no longer cyanotic. His oxygen saturation, with entubation, was a hundred percent! I stared at the monitor and realized that he had never in his life had such a high reading, such a normal reading.

Kyle opened his eyes and we rushed to his side.

"Are you okay?" Wayne asked. Kyle nodded, unable to speak due to the tube in his throat.

"Can we get you anything?" I asked. He shook his head in a negative response. He seemed alert but in pain. We stayed until supper, when his nurse increased his sedation for the night. Wayne cuddled close to Kyle and told him he loved him. Kyle mouthed the words "I love you," because he couldn't talk.

Wayne put his arm around me and guided me out of the hospital. At home, we collapsed on the couch in the basement and watched some mindless television before going to bed. I couldn't wait to see Kyle in the morning.

Kyle was extubated early in the morning. The lady from surgery, whose son had been through the same thing as Kyle, had left a stuffed bear that had a beating, battery-powered heart. A note read, "A friend gave me this when my son had his Fontan. Good luck."

He was taken off all medications except morphine. He still had his chest tube drains, which were painful. When we arrived, Kyle was bubbling to speak.

"I want my pants," he said. He was wearing a diaper and was embarrassed. Then he said, "I want to get out of here." I told him that he had to stay until he was healed. They had to make sure his new heart was perfect before they let him go home.

Then he wanted juice and we began to supply him with ice chips, lots of ice chips, as juice was still off-limits. We finally received permission to give him juice and Wayne asked him, "What kind do you want?" He replied, "Cranberry." They had none and when we passed this information along to Kyle he began to cry. He then fell asleep. Wayne rushed out to buy some and

Kyle had it when he woke up. It was a real struggle to keep him in bed because he wanted to get the drink for himself. Wendy came and he finished the entire bottle by the end of her visit. At the end of the day he had a bath and a tummy ache. Annie said, "It's the chest tubes, after they take them out he'll feel so much better." I kissed his head and he kissed me good night.

After three days Kyle began to lose weight. Oherwise, he was stable. He began to make excellent progress. His chest tubes were still draining so well that the doctors began to talk about transferring him to the ward. Their main concern was keeping up his fluids and allowing him to be comfortable. After a week, he was sent to the ward and I assumed more of his care.

My parents came by the first morning we moved back to 7C. I was resting in my rocking chair and was glad to see them. My mother had made an appointment for me for a massage, and my father dropped me off in front of the massage parlour that afternoon.

I entered the office and was welcomed by the sweet smell of incense and restful, soothing music. A tiny woman with wiry muscles exposed by her tank top and black leggings approached me. She had loose, curly dark-brown hair and a pretty face devoid of makeup. She instructed me to lie on mats on the floor.

Three candles burned on the teak table in the corner and Indian batik prints hung in the two windows. As she began to dig into my muscles and work out the kinks she said that after everything my mother had told her about Kyle, she had expected me to be exhausted. "But all your chi is flowing smoothly," she said, "you have no energy blocked at all. You are like a warrior."

High praise indeed, but I certainly felt less than Amazonian. She pushed and pummeled and even hurt me, yet after falling into a dreamlike state and seeing a kaleidoscope of colours, I felt refreshed and renewed.

Kyle had a respiratory therapist come in every morning and received a device that he had to blow into at regular intervals throughout the day. I had to force him to do his exercises, as each blow was a painful episode in itself. I also had to walk him for short, ever-increasing distances at least twice a day. The tubes coming out of every part of his chest were intolerable. When I got him out of bed, I could barely look at him as he stood there in his underwear and dressing gown. His knees looked like two knobby balls centred on two sticks. His muscles had apparently vanished. Every step that I made him take caused us both anguish. I was hard-pressed not to cry. It was pitiful to watch him painfully limp and force his recuperating body to move. Yet each day carried us slightly farther until we had made it out into the hall. Each blow in the respiratory therapist's inhaler brought us closer to the door. He was so brave I was in awe of his spirit.

Mike brought Matthew for two visits and each reunion was joyful. Though it hurt him to hug his big brother, he managed a slight embrace and many kisses. Matthew would sit with Kyle and they would tell private jokes and share sibling confidences. Mike was a tad uncomfortable, and after a perfunctory visit he would declare that visiting time was over. After giving Kyle a royal wave, Mike would whisk Matthew back to his place and I would wait for Wayne to come back. Wayne preferred to go for coffee when my ex was in the room and would sense when it was safe to return.

"Is he gone?" were the first words out of his mouth after one such encounter.

"He's in the washroom," I answered," and I'm running away with him to Tahiti."

Ten days post-op saw the removal of his right chest tube and they were considering taking out the left one on the next day. The following day that tube was still draining, so in it stayed. Two weeks after the surgery, all findings were "very satisfactory," except for the remaining left chest tube. Kyle was suffering so much due to that thing and had absolutely no appetite. He wouldn't even eat the candy I offered him in desperation.

On February 7, the surgeon's consultation led to his pacer wires coming out. On February 11, his drain slowed down so much that his lung collapsed. They put him on suction, but that didn't work. The doctors and nurses working around my son ordered me to leave the room.

I anxiously waited for news. I could imagine his screams in the next room. Why else would they have gotten rid of me? Finally, on February 13, the last drain was tossed in the garbage.

With his appetite restored, Kyle wanted a salad. We were happy to oblige him, but when the kitchen sent up their version of a mid-winter salad, we ordered out. He relished every bite and wanted more, but Wayne told him to take it easy, since he hadn't eaten in three weeks and his stomach was the size of a pea. Kyle responded by asking for the candy I had promised him. The surgery hadn't dimmed his memory in the least.

What the last three weeks had dimmed was my love life, and the next day was Valentine's Day. After work, Wayne came by as usual, but instead of spending four or five hours with Kyle, he played with him for about an hour and asked me out for dinner.

He took me to a restaurant near our home called The Vieux St. Charles. We were shown to a table for two near the centre of the room. We sat down and Wayne covered my hand with his large, bony one. I looked at his knuckles, strong and white where the ligaments strained to escape from the skin. I looked at his chewed up nails, which were chewed until they could be chewed no more. Still, he persisted in gnawing on his fingertips. He ordered for both of us, as I couldn't even be bothered to look at the menu. My tiredness felt like it seeped from deep inside and slowly, pervasively engulfed me.

We sat in silence and eavesdropped on the next table. There were four men sitting in formal business attire. Two of the gentlemen were Texans, judging from their accents and western-style suits, and the third sounded like a New Yorker. The host, a French-Canadian local, was dwarfed by the two Southerners. The talk grew louder and we were engaged and entertained by it throughout our meal.

I apologized to Wayne for not having anything to say. I was beat, worn out from everything. Wayne understood.

"Anything I could have said would have been far less interesting than their conversation," he said. "We've got a whole lifetime of Valentine's days to spend together and this one wasn't a total loss. Kyle is well and he'll be discharged in a couple of days. Then this will all be over." He took a sip of his Irish coffee. "Then we can get on with the rest of our lives."

I let out a deep sigh and felt a sense of serenity pervade my body. We could move on, Kyle would grow up and we could just maybe, hopefully, have a regular life. A life filled with the usual bumps and bruises, joys and disappointments.

I wanted some peace. I even wanted boring.

EPILOGUE:
ONE BIG HAPPY
FAMILY

After the surgery, after weeks of caring for Kyle's wound, after years of living with the constant stress of having a child that may die, we all began to heal. Our life began to take on a soothing rhythm. We were becoming an ordinary family with the extraordinary events of the past ten years, at last, slowly becoming a memory. Kyle's third birthday, shortly after his discharge, was a joyous event. His head was still shaved, but the hair had started to grow back with a fringe of stubble that covered his pate. He seemed so mature and controlled as he received his guests and his many presents. He said "thank you" to everyone for every gift, including socks. After his third pair, as he was opening another package, he commented, "My hope it not socks." I began to think about having another baby. I wanted a healthy girl this time.

I mounted my campaign three months later with a sumptuous dinner by candlelight *chez nous*, flowers and a bottle of champagne. Wayne knew something was up when he opened the front door, smelled the roast beef and heard the sound of no children. After the usual questions about our respective days, we ate in relative silence.

"Do you think, now that Kyle is okay, that we could maybe think about having a daughter?" I asked nervously. "I mean, I think it would be a girl, don't you?"

Wayne looked at me coolly. I knew he suspected I was trying to manipulate him again to get what I wanted.

"I think we should wait," he said. "Let's enjoy Kyle for now." Wayne cast down his eyes and focused on the food in front of him, hoping, I'm sure, that I would drop the subject.

"But I'll be forty in two years," I said. "My clock is ticking like a bomb."

With infinite patience, borne of years of being my soul-mate, he said, "You'll just have to try not to explode, cause I'm not ready yet. I have too much on my plate."

As far as I knew, Wayne always had too much on his plate. I would just have to convince him. Pleading wouldn't work. Begging had never swayed him in the past. I would have to come up with a new tactic.

I was off the pill, but Wayne was a very careful Capricorn. I tried getting him very drunk but he was cautious even under the influence. After a frustrating year of wheedling, I began to get depressed. When I was at work I was thinking about a baby, and when I was home I was obsessed. This unsatisfactory status quo had begun to grind me down when I noticed that my period was six days late.

It was Mother's Day, a fitting day to take a pregnancy test and tell Wayne the results over a drink. They were negative and I menstruated a few hours later. I descended into a black hole. I felt as if I couldn't speak to any one and I certainly couldn't bear to hear what they had to say. I went to work the next day and the next and by Thursday I had hit my bottom. I hadn't spoken to Wayne in days and the children had only gotten monosyllabic answers to their urgent inquiries.

I lay in bed half-conscious and listened to the sounds of the birds outside. A cacophony of birdcalls bombarded my ears. Considering the state I was in, my usual reaction would have been to stomp to the window and slam it shut, guaranteeing a sweltering sleep for the remainder of the morning, before I had to rise and shine.

Suddenly, I realized that the music outside was just that – music – and that I was being serenaded by nature. I could almost hear every leaf as it twirled and danced to the tune. I felt empowered and very small. I was overwhelmed by emotion as I accepted that I was indeed powerless. I had no control, I was not in charge. I could no better decide to have a baby and then have one than I could hop to Cleveland. I surrendered to my higher power. I gave in, I gave up and I felt pure release. I was able to be myself and have complete faith and trust that I was being cared for. It was almost as if God had picked me up and placed me in his two hands, like the old Allstate Insurance commercial. I felt buffeted by gentle pillows and knew with certainty that everything would be all right. Perfect even. Everything that would happen after this awakening would be perfect. I floated out of bed and thanked God. Who else was I going to thank?

I finally understood. It was His will, not mine. I went to work and apologized to my boss for my terrible attitude of the past week. I called Wayne and asked for forgiveness and vowed to make it up to my family. The next day, Wayne called and said, "How about we try for a baby?"

Whenever I let go and let God, I have been amazed by how quickly things have fallen into place. Since that special day in May 1997, I have had a profound shift in perspective and have developed an attitude of gratitude. I have lived my days with acceptance of what is, without expectation of what will be, and have banished guilt and stress from my life.

My third son was born March 9, 1998. We named him Quinn Brody Rooney. He would have been Brody Quinn Rooney, except that I was in labour as we rounded the corner to the hospital and would have agreed to anything Wayne asked of me. Clever boy, he sure could pick his moments.

We stayed in a birthing room for the entire delivery and even with two births behind me, I had been uncertain about when to leave for the hospital. The room was gaily painted yellow and the bed was comfortable and extremely practical, in that it could convert into a delivery table. I needed another induction and again the contractions bombarded me immediately after the drip began. Wayne paced nervously. He would leave the room for brief intervals to answer his cell phone, and managed to have a record-breaking sales day and a new baby at the same time. The baby moved suddenly and it felt to me, on the outside, that he had stretched full length and that a head or a foot must be sticking out.

The child slid out with relative ease and looked at me like an old Tibetan monk. I was thrilled at the moment of his birth and have been pleasantly pleased by Quinn ever since.

At six weeks of age, a photographer came to the house to take pictures of the new baby. The house was in disarray. I was slightly less so. The man was heavy set, sweaty, with every gadget and accessory that he needed hanging from his vest. He got a list of names from the hospital and then photographed every child on it, hoping for a sale. He had seen a lot of babies in his time. After he posed Quinn and snapped several pictures, the gentleman commented that he had never seen a happier baby. And this was before Quinn had eaten lunch and had a long-overdue nap. It was true. Quinn smiled the entire time and never made a fuss. He was similarly good-natured when we went for a week to New Hampshire in June and slept twelve-hour nights and took two long naps a day.

When Quinn was eighteen months old he had a fever. I took him to the doctor, who advised me to take him to the hospital.

Now these are words I could barely stand to hear. With a heavy heart I went and sat in the same room in emergency where Matthew had undergone his painful spinal tap fourteen years earlier. I forced myself not to

cringe or cry as the staff carried out their endless barrage
of tests. Two hours later I waited in a cubicle for the
news that my child had a devastating, rare defect and
that they would have to operate. But three time's a
charm. The doctor moved the curtain, patted Quinn on
the head, and said, "He's fine, you can take him home."

I could not understand what she had just said. It was
as if she was speaking in Swahili. I staggered blindly out
to the car with my precious, healthy son. He has had one
ear infection and two runny noses in the subsequent
seven years. He has medium brown hair, brown eyes (he
was my last hope for passing on Wayne's blue peepers)
and is tall for his age. He is clever, a quick reader, and
writes in cursive better than both his older brothers.
Quinn is a singer and loves to dance and tell jokes. He
has broken his leg, cracked open his head (five stitches)
and stubs his toe from May to September in his black
flip-flops. He is an absolute joy and is rarely in a bad
mood. He is one of the happiest people I know.

Over five years ago, when Quinn was almost three,
we moved from the suburbs of Montreal to the Eastern
Townships, just north of the Vermont-Canada border.
We bought a ramshackle one hundred and seventy-five-
year-old Victorian manor in Knowlton and have been
renovating ever since. We have done the kitchen and two
new bathrooms as well as the master bedroom in the last
two years. Wayne was never content just painting and
installing new cupboard doors. He gutted rooms and
even replaced exterior walls in the restoration. I had no
real kitchen and no functioning bathtub for the first

three years we lived in our home, but the results have been well worth it.

Kyle is almost fourteen and is tall and handsome. He has dirty blond hair that he is trying to grow long like the other boys, but is having trouble convincing his parents. He is attending grade eight in a French high school in the International Baccalaureate program. He is one of only three anglophones out of three hundred students. He is a B student except for gym class, where despite his best efforts, he has been saddled with a C. He is studying the guitar and learning German with my mother, as she plans to take him to Germany next year. He wears glasses and has braces to correct an overbite. He is funny, smart and has a quick temper. He tells me he loves me several times a day, and astonishingly, hugs me almost as often. He takes blood pressure medicine twice a day and an aspirin every morning. Kyle loves video games and has to be given limits or he would play into the night. He reads a lot and wants to be a writer. He is developing well physically, emotionally, intellectually and spiritually. He is an incredible person and I feel honoured to know him.

Matthew is twenty-one, of legal age, and has lived away from home since he turned seventeen. Due to a lack of English facilities in rural areas, anglophone children are forced to move to Montreal to continue their education. Matthew has been living with his father and is just finishing CJEP in the Commerce program. He hopes to attend the John Molson School of Business at Concordia University, but needs to improve his marks before he is accepted. He has a brilliant mind, but never bothers studying until it is almost too late. He wears a lot of gold and has baggy pants that threaten to fall down with impunity. He is six-foot-three and has beautifully soft, brown hair. His features are a mix of both parents, and even if I weren't his proud mother I would have to say he's good looking.

Matthew has traveled quite a bit with his father and his stepmother; his most recent trip was to Greece. He has been seeing the same girl for a very long time and she lives with him at Mike's place. Her name is Samantha and we all love her. She is petite, dark and the perfect foil for Matthew. She is a dancer, painter and pianist and will be studying photography at Concordia University in the fall. Matthew also tells me he loves me quite often and will always embrace me when he arrives for a visit, as he is leaving and several times in between. I had heard that boys are very affectionate with their mothers and my three sons are living proof. I try to stay out of Matthew's life and will only give advice if asked. He doesn't ask much, so I've left him to find his own way. That's all any one of us really has when you come down to it. He seems to be managing, and if he's happy and a good person, that's all that matters to me. We don't agree on many philosophies, but we agree that each is entitled to his or her own opinions, and I don't try to change his. I've found that not being judgmental often keeps the door of communication open a tiny crack.

Not judging others is one of my fundamental priorities. Forgiveness for others is another way to free myself and banish fear. I found that prayer or sending a white light to a person that has tried to hurt you is incredibly uplifting. I try not to allow other people to affect my mood, my behavior or my general outlook on life. If someone is determined to have a bad day, I am equally determined not to be sucked into their vortex of fear and dis-ease. I try to stay calm and have a sense of the beauty all around me, and sometimes I fail in a grandiose manner.

I call in to radio stations frequently and win all the time. My largest prize so far was an all-expenses paid trip to Toronto. One recent Saturday morning, I called in to a travel show to win a trip for two to France. I knew with certainty that I would be the one chosen at the end of the show. That was when the winner selected would be called back, on air, and would have to answer with a pre-determined phrase of their choosing. Meanwhile Wayne kept coming in the house and asking for the phone, and trailing leaves and debris and dirt.

Just when I was chewing him out about the mess he was making on my clean floor, unbeknownst to me, the hosts were about to call the winner. The phone rang, and in an effort to get whoever was calling off the line so the travel show could call, I answered the phone with a curt hello. I was hysterical when they cut me off because I hadn't said the right greeting. I grabbed Wayne by the collar and, in front of the children, screamed, "This is all your bloody fault." I hurled myself up and down the hallway, yelling. Finally I threw myself in the shower to cool off. This was not serene behavior

I've had three gynecological surgeries in the last three years to fix a fistula that developed following Kyle's difficult birth. Each one entailed not walking or having sex for weeks, and all have failed. I fell down the stairs two years ago at work and required twenty-three stitches on my right forearm and suffered a broken wrist, a twisted neck and back, and a concussion that has left me with post-concussion syndrome. This has given me faulty short-term memory, which I must explain over and over when I disappoint others by forgetting their names or an appointment.

My marriage is not perfect and my life is far from perfect but in a way they are both perfect. In that everything unfolds exactly as it should and therefore is exactly right. I may or may not be seeing myself clearly, but I try to be mindful and to follow a spiritual path with meditation, creative visualization, reading and stabs at Buddhism.

I have always said that if I could give Kyle a pill that would make him have a normal heart I would not give it to him, because his heart is perfect for him and made him who he is right now and our family unit what it is today. Acceptance of what is and being in the moment have allowed me an unimaginable freedom. I have serenity most of the time and, of course, like everyone else I lose it occasionally. Sometimes even in a spectacular way that upon reflection was rather bad form. But I try to recover quickly, step back into being aware, mindful if only momentarily, and to go on, one day at a time. We are all one. Love each other because in the end, that's all there is. Love.

MEMBER OF SCABRINI GROUP

Québec, Canada
2006